THE
FEARLESS LIFE

THE
FEARLESS LIFE

JENTEZEN FRANKLIN

CHARISMA
HOUSE

Most CHARISMA HOUSE BOOK GROUP products
are available at special quantity discounts for bulk
purchase for sales promotions, premiums, fund-raising,
and educational needs. For details, write Charisma
House Book Group, 600 Rinehart Road, Lake Mary,
Florida 32746, or telephone (407) 333-0600.

THE FEARLESS LIFE by Jentezen Franklin
Published by Charisma House
Charisma Media/Charisma House Book Group
600 Rinehart Road
Lake Mary, Florida 32746
www.charismahouse.com

Unless otherwise noted, all Scripture quotations
are from the New King James Version of the Bible.
Copyright © 1979, 1980, 1982 by Thomas Nelson, Inc.,
publishers. Used by permission.

Scripture quotations marked KJV are from the King
James Version of the Bible.

Scripture quotations marked NIV are from the
Holy Bible, New International Version of the Bible.

Cover design by Justin Evans
Design Director: Bill Johnson

Visit the author's website at www.jentezenfranklin.org.

Library of Congress Cataloging-in-Publication Data:
Franklin, Jentezen, 1962-
  The fearless life / Jentezen Franklin.
     pages cm
  Includes bibliographical references.
  ISBN 978-1-62136-549-5 (trade paper) -- ISBN 978-1-62136-584-6 (ebook)
  1. Problem solving--Religious aspects--Christianity. 2. Confidence--Religious aspects--Christianity. I. Title.
  BV4599.5.P75F73 2014
  248.8'6--dc23
                                    2013032518

Portions of this book were previously published as *Fear Fighters* by Charisma House, ISBN 978-1-59979-762-5, copyright © 2009, and *Believe That You Can* by Charisma House, ISBN 978-1-59979-348-1, copyright © 2008.

While the author has made every effort to provide accurate telephone numbers and Internet addresses at the time of publication, neither the publisher nor the author assumes any responsibility for errors or for changes that occur after publication.

14 15 16 17 18 — 9 8 7 6 5 4 3 2 1
Printed in the United States of America

There is no fear in love;
but perfect love casts out all fear.
—1 JOHN 4:18

CONTENTS

INTRODUCTION

D O YOU WORRY too much?

Fear has gripped America. We see it in the economy; in challenges with our health care system; in politics; in rising unemployment levels, diseases, and crime; in increasing acts of terrorism; and conflicts around the world. Every day our news media bring us stories designed to make us more afraid. We live in a world that seems to be getting scarier by the day.

To make matters worse, most of us add to these real concerns with a laundry list of personal worries and fears about things that may or may not even be rational. How much energy and emotion have you wasted fearing things that never materialize? Some research suggests that only about 8 percent of everything we worry about actually has the possibility of happening![1]

I've written this book because it is not God's will for your life to be ruled by fear of any kind. You were meant to live the fearless life. That's why I'm giving you the tools you need to overcome the most common fears all of us face at one time or another: fear of failure, fear of rejection from other people, fear of not having enough, fear about bad things happening to your family or your health, and fear of death.

Living the fearless life doesn't mean you'll never feel afraid, but it does mean you can face that fear and overcome it to take God-inspired risks and succeed. You can feel secure knowing God Almighty is your refuge. You can live with courage in every situation you face!

Don't settle for a life ruled by fear, a life where the enemy has stolen your joy, peace, and future. Here's an amusing little poem to give you a picture of the kind of life I want you to avoid.

> There was a very cautious man
> Who never laughed or played;
> He never risked, he never tried,
> He never sang or prayed.
> And when he one day passed away
> His insurance was denied;
> For since he never really lived,
> They claimed he never died![2]

What a zero! I don't want to get to the end of my life and realize that I left any part of it untapped because of fear. Since you've picked up this book, I'm praying you feel the same way.

It's impossible to live life without feeling any fear at all, but the kind of fear that controls you and steals your very life from you doesn't come from God. The Bible says, "For God has not given us a spirit of fear, but of power and of love and of a sound mind" (2 Tim. 1:7).

God has given you everything you need to defeat your fears. With His help you can be everything He created you to be. Join me on this journey to discover all the weapons in His arsenal for defeating your fears and living the fearless life!

1

LIVING the FEARLESS LIFE

FOR SEVERAL YEARS I traveled as an evangelist, speaking an average of six nights a week in different churches. During that time I perfected a basic repertoire of about thirty sermons, which I'd preached so often that had I dropped dead in the middle of any of them, my wife could have finished them for me. So, when I was asked to become the pastor of Free Chapel, I faced the challenge of preparing three new sermons each week. My greatest fear was that I couldn't do it. Did I have what it takes to stay fresh, grow my congregation, and build a strong pulpit ministry? Looking back, I see God's wisdom at work. He placed me in a small community where I could do the least amount of damage while still learning.

Every weekend the challenge came back. By

Tuesday the pressure began to build as I approached Sunday. Often I'd study until 2:00 a.m. or 3:00 a.m. on Sunday morning and leave my office feeling drained and apprehensive, praying, "Lord, if You don't help me this morning, I'm sunk!"

But I learned to swim. I became a reader, discovered great resources, developed discipline and solid study habits, and above all, I learned to lean on God as never before. That lesson of learning to lean on God is the way I overcame one of the biggest fears in my life. It was the first step in living out a concept I'm talking about in this book called "the fearless life." And it is the key for you as you face whatever situation you're in right now that has caused you to pick up this book.

You know what they say about fear? FEAR = **F**alse **E**vidence **A**ppearing **R**eal. Fear comes in two basic categories:

1. Fear that you won't get what you need

2. Fear that you won't be able to hold on to what you have

Anybody who ever beat the odds or made a difference did it in spite of their fear. They did it because they were desperate and felt like they didn't have a choice. Sometimes they were inspired by somebody else's example. They said, "If not me, then who? If not now, when?" They didn't think much about it at all, or else they might have changed their mind.

What are you waiting for—a feeling of courage? Forget it! It doesn't exist. You're only courageous when you do what's right despite your fears! That courage in the face of your fears is how I'm defining fearlessness. You'll still feel the uncomfortable situation you're in, but you'll also feel the freedom of knowing God will handle it, so you have nothing to fear. That's the fearless life.

The Bible is a David-and-Goliath book. It teaches you that with God on your side, you're bigger than any problem, so you can be fearless. The question is, do you believe that enough to step out and allow God to use you? If you're just believing God for things you can do for yourself, you're limiting Him. Furthermore, if you think He'll never ask you to do things you can't do, think again! Jesus told one man to walk on water and another to come out of his grave—and they did!

Instead of focusing on what you're afraid of,

recognize that God has called you and equipped you, accept the gifts He's given you, and start building on them.

LET GOD CHALLENGE YOU

Whatever season you are in, God wants you to learn to say, "I cannot do this in my own strength. I need to lean on Him." You'll never have all the answers, so you might as well leave the risk-free "safe zone," where you can figure out the next step and can handle whatever comes your way, in favor of living in the faith zone.

Living the fearless life requires living in the faith zone. It means reaching up and grabbing hold of nothing and holding on to it until it becomes something. God wants you to live there. In fact, He wants you to live there so much that He will stretch you again and again. (He'll let you stay in your safe zone for a while if you need to, but He really does not want you to *live* there.)

Let God challenge you to step out on nothing. Even if you're not particularly desperate at the moment, allow yourself to become willing to take a faith risk just because He is calling you. When you move out into the faith zone, when you choose to live the fearless life, you'll discover that's where God *lives.*

I would not be writing this to you if I had chosen to live my life in the safe zone. When I had been an evangelist for a while, I was in the safe zone. I was in my denomination. Cherise and I were traveling and ministering. We were doing fine, and we had a dependable salary. We felt that we had a good future and that everything was looking up. But right in the midst of that security and everything going right, God's Spirit began to agitate me and stir me up with tremendous discontent.

I found myself absolutely miserable, even though I had everything (I thought). God's Spirit began to touch me, and He said, "Are you ready to move out of the safe zone into the faith zone? You can stay here, and it will be OK, but you'll never get to see the miracles, you'll never get to see the supernatural, you'll never get to see what I really could have done in your life—unless you'll dare to get out of that safe zone and step into the faith zone."

I'm so glad I said yes to His invitation! We went from doing good things to being in God's perfect will, and there's a big difference between those two. Now, I need to tell you that if you're in God's perfect will, you may find yourself feeling very unsafe at times. You will feel extremely uncomfortable. But you will learn to depend on the Lord as you never could learn back in the comfort of your safe zone. Remember, when a God-given opportunity comes along, it is God's gift to you. What you do with that opportunity is your gift to God.

You need to understand something about God. The Bible says, "Without faith it is impossible to please Him" (Heb. 11:6). That means that it does not matter how much religious activity is going on in your life. If you are not relying on your faith, you are not pleasing God.

If you're in the safe zone, you don't really have to pray and seek God for anything because you feel OK about what you have already. You don't really have to be anointed because you can do everything without the anointing. Even though the security of the safe zone is what we try to achieve our whole life long, it's not God's will for His children. His will is that

> When a God-given opportunity comes along, it is God's gift to you. What you do with that opportunity is your gift to God.

His children will always be dependent upon Him. Always.

If you want to be where God is, break out of the risk-free safe zone and start living in the faith zone. It's risky, but the faith zone is where God lives!

The faith zone is where miracles happen. You'll never see a "Red Sea" part as long as you stay back in the safe zone. You'll never see manna come supernaturally from heaven. You'll never see the miraculous things God wants to do in your life— the exceedingly, abundantly, above-all-you-can-ask-or-think things—as long as you have it "made in the shade." So the first step in living the fearless life is putting yourself in a place where God *has* to come through for you or it's all over.

You may feel that you've heard this message before, and it didn't work for you. You tried taking a risk, you tried walking on water, and you sank like a stone. Look at Moses. There he was, eighty years old, and he'd already spent forty years in the wilderness, looking after sheep. His life looked like a pretty complete failure. He thought he'd heard God the last time, and look what happened. And then a burning bush strikes up a conversation with him.

God didn't seem to be restricted by Moses's

limited opinion of the matter. He doesn't usually need somebody who's super-duper prepared and super-duper intelligent. He just needs somebody who'll lean on Him, somebody like Moses, who says, "Yes, Sir, I'll obey, but I can't do it by myself." There he was with all his problems and insecurities—not the least of which was his advanced age—and God helped him to do the impossible.

As long as you stay in the safe zone, you're not going to grow. You can't stay the same and learn at the same time. Many people have been saved, and they're safe from hell. They're on the way to heaven, no question about it. That's fine. But maybe there's more than that. Maybe God is knocking at their door, trying to get their attention, so they'll step out of their safe little houses and step into the baptism of the Holy Spirit and a whole lot more.

Many are so afraid to risk anything that they just stay behind closed doors. It's like they live their entire lives in Egypt, in the land of "not enough." Some people break out and take one step of faith—and they wind up in the wilderness, the land of "just enough." If they continue in a forward direction, living by faith, the day will come when they will enter the promised land. It's the land of milk and honey, a land where the harvest is so great it will boggle your mind. It's a land of more than enough. It's a land where you're walking in the faith zone all the time, so when mountains get in the way, God moves them; when oceans get in the way, God parts them. It's worth putting in some wilderness time to get there, and it's worth the discomfort of being stretched.

> As long as you stay in the safe zone, you're not going to grow. You can't stay the same and learn at the same time.

Anytime believers step out of the safety of the old, comfortable way and start to trust God's provision, they have to deal with a huge factor of the unknown. Look how Paul phrased it when he told the elders from the church at Ephesus where he was going next: "And now, behold, I go bound in the spirit unto Jerusalem, *not knowing* the things that shall befall me there" (Acts 20:22, KJV, emphasis added). "Not knowing," he was going anyway. He didn't know whether he would be received or killed. All he knew was that he was in the will of God. He knew he was bound in the Holy Spirit to make the trip. He didn't know anything beyond that. He was walking into the situation blind. That's living by faith. That's the fearless life.

FACING OFF WITH YOUR FEARS

It was a typical Sunday afternoon in late January. I had finished preaching that morning in my church in Gainesville, Georgia, and was preparing to board a plane with my wife, two of our children, and some staff from our church. We were flying to our pastorate in California to preach to several thousand people who would attend two services later that afternoon. This Sunday afternoon flight to California had become a happy routine since God had opened the door for us to pastor Free Chapel Orange County, our West Coast campus. However, this Sunday would be anything but routine.

Every January at Free Chapel we begin the year with a twenty-one-day fast. This particular Sunday was special since it was the last day of the fast—which meant we could eat!

We had just begun enjoying our meal when suddenly the cabin of the plane became extremely hot. We reached up to open the air vents, and smoke billowed. Next thing we knew, one of the pilots came out of the cockpit to urge us to put on our masks and brace ourselves because we were on our way down for an emergency landing due to a loss of pressure.

That's when everybody started throwing out their lunch. But not me; this was my first meal in twenty-one days! If this was my final day on this earth, I wasn't going to leave it hungry! I asked the person next to me to pass the ketchup, and I kept on eating. I had one hand on my wife's knee to calm her down, the other hand holding my fork, and my elbow steadying my plate.

Sure, I was scared at the thought that something was terribly wrong, but in the midst of my fear, I had peace. Though it was a terrifying situation, I had a calmness in my spirit, and I knew that everything was going to be all right. It wasn't until we landed and the emergency trucks rushed the plane that I realized the magnitude of the situation. I began to praise the Lord for His protection, and I proclaimed to the enemy that he had lost again.

The next week when we were getting ready to board the plane, fear confronted me. In that moment I had a decision to make: fight the fear and get on board, or give in to fear and give up on God's assignment for my life. That day my prayer before liftoff was much more earnest than in the past. I began to quote Psalm 91 and claim God's promise of protection. I chose to fight my fear instead of allowing fear to conquer me. And each week I continue to get on that plane and fly across the country to minister to thousands of people.

I learned a lesson that day. Whenever fear comes my way—and it will come—I have a choice. My faith can fight fear. I don't have to panic and get myself worked up in frightening situations. If I stay focused on God's promise and allow faith to fight fear, He will keep me in perfect peace.

LIVING WITHOUT FEAR

As I considered that phenomenal peace I experienced in what should have been a frightening situation, I began to meditate on the scriptures that promise us a life without fear:

> For God has not given us a spirit of fear, but of power and of love and of a sound mind.
>
> —2 TIMOTHY 1:7

Overcoming fear is something we all face when we endeavor to do new things, such as take a new job, fall in love, create a new product line, or start a business. In short, there can be no progress in life without taking risks. We cannot succeed in life if we give in to fear.

If you do not face off with your fears, they will keep you from living the victorious life that God meant for you. And you will suffer the regret of what could have, would have, or should have been.

You will never be perfect. So you will never be perfectly successful. That doesn't mean you will not succeed in life—but you must try.

AFRAID TO TRY?

I heard of a guy who couldn't speak English. He was terrified of trying because he did not want to fail. So he found an English teacher and asked him to teach him how to order a meal in a restaurant in perfect English. The teacher taught him how to say four words: hamburger, french fries, and Coke.

Every day after that, the man went to order his hamburger, french fries, and Coke. Soon he grew tired of eating the same thing every day. So he asked the English teacher to teach him how to order something else to eat. The teacher taught him to say eggs, toast, and juice.

So the man went happily to the restaurant to order eggs, toast, and juice. But when the waiter asked,

"How do you want your eggs?" the guy stared back blankly. Then the waiter asked, "What kind of toast do you want? And would you like orange juice or apple juice?" The guy stared helplessly at the waiter for a moment and then said, "Hamburger, french fries, Coke."

A lot of people live a "hamburger, french fries, Coke" life because they are not willing to do something imperfectly or try to do something new. They will not face off with their fears and risk failure. Their answer to risk-taking is to play it safe. But you cannot please God by playing it safe, and you cannot succeed in life without taking risks.

Does this apply to something in your life right now? Is there a way that you've held back out of fear of failure or fear of suffering? Have you tried to keep yourself all tucked up in your little safe zone so that you don't have to be vulnerable ever again? Maybe you've been through a divorce and you just don't want to trust anyone ever again. Maybe it's something else. Whatever it is, take a long, hard look at it. Hold it up against some of the scriptures that promise us a life without fear. Remember Paul and Moses and all of the other people who took risks and stepped out of their ruts.

Open yourself up to the Holy Spirit and pray this prayer with me:

> *Heavenly Father, I want to give You my fears. I turn my whole life over to You. I want to live in faith. I believe; help my unbelief! Fill me with courage, and furnish me with faith. I need it. I want to walk in Your will.*

2

FEARLESS ABOUT FAILURE

FAILURE. THERE IS hardly a more terrifying word in the human language. Failing economy, failing marriage, failing grades, failing to fulfill your dreams. The fear of failure is so paralyzing that it keeps many people from even reaching for their dreams; they simply cannot face the risk of trying and failing.

What is keeping you from living your dream? Are you afraid to risk failure to walk in destiny? You can only live the fearless life when you expect to walk in the success God has for you. Only then can you live in His purpose and destiny where you will know ultimate fulfillment in life.

Fear of failure is listed among the top ten worst human fears. It ranks alongside other "learned" fears that include the fear of public speaking, rejection, disapproval, making mistakes, aloneness, financial problems, and death.[1]

Did you know that there are over two thousand fears or phobias that have been identified in human experience? Yet, according to psychologists, human beings are born with just two basic fears: the fear of loud noises and the fear of falling. All other fears have to be learned.[2]

That means you were not born with a fear of failure. You learned to be afraid of failing because of what you have experienced in life. Failure was not God's intention for mankind. Fear entered the human race because of sin.

The first thing Adam did after he sinned was run and hide from the presence of God. When God came to commune with him in the cool of the day, Adam was nowhere to be found. God called to him, and Adam answered, "I heard Your voice in the garden, and *I was afraid* because I was naked; and I hid myself" (Gen. 3:10, emphasis added).

The primary evil that Satan released into the earth through sin was fear. Now people suffer the torment of all kinds of fears that paralyze them, robbing them of a victorious life. Fear will keep you from trying because you might fail. You might look foolish, or you might be rejected.

Do you remember the Michael Jackson album *Thriller*? This hit song and music video is listed in the Guinness Book of Records (2006) as the most successful music video. It focuses on the fear of the thriller movies. Why was it so popular? There are many reasons, but I believe at least one of the reasons people liked it so much is because it was centered on fear, and everybody can relate to fear.

SCARY MOMENTS CAN BE GREAT OPPORTUNITIES

Some of my scariest moments have given me my greatest opportunities. When the Lord called me to preach, I was traveling with my brother, who was preaching as an evangelist. He invited me to preach one night of the revival services where he was ministering. For an entire week before that opportunity, I was so nervous and frightened that I became sick.

You will not meet a shyer, more backward and introverted person than I was at that time. My heart pounded just to think of getting up in front of people. I fasted and prayed that week, and I still remember the terror I felt that day when we got into the car and my brother drove me to that service where I was to preach my first sermon.

I was agonizing in the passenger seat, thinking something like, "This is not happening. It is simply not happening." Here I was about to get up in front of forty people and preach. It might as well have been forty thousand people, as frightened as I was. My mind was racing. I thought to myself, "What do you think you are doing? You won't remember a word you are supposed to preach." I was sure that I was going to look foolish. What if I failed?

The pastor of the church introduced me and announced that I was coming to preach my first sermon. I was cringing in my seat, afraid that I was going to embarrass myself and look stupid. But I defied my fear. I preached that sermon. It was a pitiful sermon, but years later I realized that by overcoming one of my scariest moments, I had stepped into my greatest opportunity. Destiny was opened to me through that opportunity.

Some of my scariest moments occurred when I was dating my wife. I got up the courage to ask her for a date, and she accepted. I was relieved and grateful. After we had dated a few times, I realized that we were becoming seriously interested in one another. I was a traveling evangelist at the time and was ministering at a revival in Alabama. So I asked her to try to arrange to travel to the services for the weekend to see me. Her aunt and uncle offered to bring her, and the arrangements were finalized.

Before they left to come to Alabama, her mother told her that she knew I was going to tell her that I loved her during the visit with me. Of course, I did not know anything about that until later.

I had asked her to go out for dinner with me after the service, along

> By overcoming one of my scariest moments, I had stepped into my greatest opportunity.

with her aunt and uncle. Then, later that evening, we were sitting alone talking. As the conversation progressed, I took the opportunity to say to her, "I love you."

The conversation ended abruptly. She went completely silent for what seemed an eternity. Immediately I was gripped with fear. I didn't know she was in shock, thinking about what her mother had told her. I just knew that I had told her I loved her and thought that her silence meant she did not feel the same way.

So, I started to panic, thinking I must have misread her feelings and that she was going to reject my love. Quickly I tried to find a way to take back my words. I fumbled around trying to say something to put her at ease. I managed, "You know, when someone says they love you, it can mean many things, like 'I've never felt this way before' or 'I care deeply for you.' It doesn't necessarily mean that I am in love with you." I was fighting desperately for a way out of my dilemma when she interrupted me.

Through my fog of fear I heard her say, "I love you too." Relief flooded my mind and heart, and I blurted out, "OK, I really do love you." As they say, the rest is history. We have laughed many times about that moment. But what if I had given in to the fear of rejection? What if I had not risked telling her how I felt? I could have missed out on the great love of my life.

When I asked her to marry me, once again I was scared to death. I thought, "What if she has had second thoughts? What if she says no?" But she said yes, and that scary moment led to one of the best opportunities of my life—the honeymoon. We have been married for more than twenty years and have five great kids. What if I had missed all of that by giving into fear? Living the fearless life means taking advantage of opportunities.

Whether you're single or married, you can see how these examples apply to many different relationships in our lives. When is the last time you fearlessly struck up a conversation with a stranger and shared the love of Jesus with them? Have you ever freely offered your friendship to someone to see if God might use you to minister to someone's needs? In the process you might make some rewarding lifelong relationships that become a blessing to your life. You don't know what you may be missing if you allow fear of rejection to paralyze you.

Another example from my own life is when Cherise and I left the denomination where we started in ministry because God spoke to us to go to a small church in Gainesville. My mind was screaming at me to go back home and be safe in the ministry where we were comfortable. But God gave us courage to leave everything familiar that we loved to begin to minister at Free Chapel in Gainesville. God has been with us to give us good success.

Every expansion of this ministry has required

that I overcome the fear that would keep me playing it safe. Sometimes it seemed impossible to do what God had told us to do. Building facilities that cost millions of dollars to accommodate the vision God has given us requires courage. Establishing community outreaches and going to the nations has been a challenge every step of the way. Fear would have kept us from fruitfulness in these areas.

I remember when God first gave us the opportunity to add our second campus in Orange County. When I first got on the plane to fly to California, my mind was telling me that I did not know what I was doing. How could I pastor a church on the East Coast and another on the West Coast both on the same day?

Yet now the Orange County church has grown to several thousand people and involves effective outreaches to the community. If God says to do something, then you need to do it and shame the devil. Fight the fear that he tries to put in your way. When you live the fearless life, you take advantage of opportunities.

When I look back at that first sermon I preached in that little country church, I realize that message was huge. It was a gift of God to give me an opportunity to enter into destiny. Now God has given me the opportunity to preach to multitudes of people through travel and television. It all goes back to that first message I preached in one of my scariest moments.

When I remember asking my wife for our first date, I am aware that overcoming that scary moment opened a wonderful door for my future. Daring to fight my fear has resulted in life opportunities to walk in destiny that would have been lost otherwise.

What about you? I wonder what opportunities you are backing down from that God has placed in your life to promote you to unbelievable success. What have you been afraid to do that might be a God-given opportunity for your future? God wants you to take advantage of your opportunities. He wants you to experience success of unbelievable proportions if you will fight your fear and take a risk.

The odds may be against you. Family may oppose you. You may think you are being foolish, and the outcome may be questionable. But if you are waiting for a perfect time with little or no risk of failure, you will not move into your God-given destiny. It always comes with risk.

What may seem to be an insignificant opportunity, like my first sermon, could be a big doorway swinging on one little hinge—your decision to take advantage of that small opportunity.

WHAT IS YOUR CONTRIBUTION?

Thomas Edison failed at six thousand attempts to make an electric light bulb that would work. On one occasion a young journalist asked Edison why he kept trying and failing to make light by using electricity: "Don't you know that gas lights are with us to stay?" Edison replied, "I have not failed. I've just found ten thousand ways that won't work."[3]

Raymond Kroc had little success in a number of business ventures before he became acquainted with the McDonald brothers' local hamburger restaurants. He was traveling across the country, selling multimixer milkshake machines. After working with them for a while, Kroc risked everything to purchase the McDonald brothers' hamburger restaurants. He implemented Henry Ford's assembly line idea into his restaurants, changing the way hamburgers were made. Through his efforts the McDonald's golden arches were born.[4]

What would have happened to our twenty-first-century scientific progress if Thomas Edison had quit his experiments with the light bulb after ten thousand failures? How many McDonald's hamburgers and fries would you have eaten if Ray Kroc had not overcome his failure in business? They refused to accept failure and kept seeking greater opportunity for their potential success.

Will you make your contribution to the world as God intended? I believe one of the wealthiest places in the world is the graveyard. How many people have taken their potential for writing a book, composing music, curing disease, or inventing a vital instrument to the grave with them because of fear? How many people never achieve anything because they are afraid they will look foolish trying? Fear of failure makes you hide from opportunity.

How Do You Define Failure?

To fail, according to Webster, means "to fall short, to be unsuccessful, to disappoint expectations, to be inadequate or become bankrupt." According to that definition, the failure rate of the human race is 100 percent!

It is impossible as a human being to eliminate failure from your life. So the real question is: What will you do when you fail? In a relationship? In business? In reaching your personal goals? Will you give in to fear of failure and quit trying?

Living the fearless life requires you to get over your fear of failure. If you don't, you will become paralyzed at the prospect of taking a risk. The important thing to remember when you fail is not to quit. History shows that failure can actually become a catalyst to propel you to success.

> One of the wealthiest places in the world is the graveyard. How many people have taken their potential for writing, composing, curing, or inventing to the grave with them?

Napoleon was forty-second in his class of forty-three, but he led his army successfully to conquer the world. George Washington lost two-thirds of his military battles but won the Revolutionary War against overwhelming odds. Abraham Lincoln's list of failures in life exceeded his successes before he became one of the greatest presidents of the United

States in 1861. Here are some of the failures he experienced:[5]

ABRAHAM LINCOLN'S FAILURES

1832—Defeated for state legislature
1833—Failed in business
1835—Sweetheart died
1836—Had nervous breakdown
1838—Defeated for Illinois House Speaker
1843—Defeated for nomination for Congress
1848—Lost renomination
1854—Defeated for US Senate
1856—Defeated for nomination for vice president
1858—Again defeated for US Senate

Albert Einstein was considered a dunce and told to switch from his studies in physics to some other subject. Today his name is synonymous with the term *genius*. He is credited with discovering the theory of relativity and is called the Father of the Atomic Age. The scientific community calls him the greatest scientist since Sir Isaac Newton.[6]

When you think of George Washington, Abraham Lincoln, or Albert Einstein, you probably do not remember their failures. You remember their contributions to the world. Yet, how would history be changed if their successes had been aborted because they quit when they first failed?

You need to realize that failure is not final. The

Bible says that a righteous man may fall seven times and will rise again (Prov. 24:16). And failure is not fatal. You can begin again after failure. It is the fear of failure that could prove fatal to your goals in life. Fear will keep you from trying again.

In baseball, the superstars fail to hit the ball 70 percent of the time. If they maintain a batting average of three hundred or better, they are considered the best in the game. That means that for every one thousand times they come to bat, they will fail to get on base seven hundred times. These athletic champions have to live with that enormous rate of failure every day.

Roger Bannister, a young medical student at Oxford, wanted to be a part of the track team. He worked hard to become fit. And in 1952 he ran in the Olympics and failed to win. He did not finish higher than fourth place and failed to earn a medal. But Roger Bannister did not quit in the face of his failure.

> You need to realize that failure is not final…and failure is not fatal. You can begin again after failure.

Experts had concluded that it was not humanly possible to run the mile in under four minutes. Yet that was Bannister's goal. And on May 6, 1954, he became the first man to run a mile in under four minutes. His time was 3 minutes 59.4 seconds. He refused to accept the experts' impossibility thinking. After Bannister's success, other athletes were inspired to break the four-minute-mile barrier as well.[7]

BENEFITS OF FAILURE

If you don't quit when you fail, you will ultimately succeed in life. When babies start learning to walk, they begin by hitting every piece of furniture in the house. They fall and get up, then fall again and get up again—until they have mastered the balance they need to walk.

Life is like that. You have to decide to keep getting up every time you fall. Keep looking forward. Don't waste your time lamenting past failure. You have goals to reach that need all of your energy. You see, true failure isn't in falling down; you only truly fail if you stop getting back up and trying again.

Failure actually has some great benefits to work in your life. Someone has wisely concluded, "It is a mistake to suppose that people succeed through success; they often succeed through failures."[8]

The psalmist said it was good for him to fail because through his failure he learned the consequences of his actions. He recognized that he was going in the wrong direction and could change it to become pleasing to God and successful in life (Ps. 119:6–7).

1. When people fail in one area, it drives them to explore other avenues of success. Most of life's successes are based on the principle of trial and error. Remember, failure is not falling short of your goal. Failure is simply not making the effort.

2. Sometimes failing will actually help you discover your area of success. For example, when you hate your job, you will likely fail in it. Yet, in losing that hated position, you may be pressed to pursue what you really like to do.

   Nathaniel Hawthorne studied to become a successful writer. However, his first novel was unsuccessful. He could not earn a living at writing, and he wanted to get married. So, Hawthorne took a job as a surveyor to pay the bills.

But he was eventually dismissed from that position. Desperate, he turned back to writing, which he loved, knowing he must make a living from it. He wrote diligently and authored his famous novel *The Scarlet Letter*. It was an immediate success. From that time on, Hawthorne was able to enjoy his coveted career as a writer.[9]

3. Another benefit to failure is that it will make you less judgmental. When you fail, you become more sympathetic with other people's failures. You don't kick people when they are down anymore, saying things like, "I don't believe they did that." You know how it hurts to fail, and you feel their pain because of what you have experienced.

Don't allow fear of failure to rob you of productivity and the joys of life. Be willing to fail and learn from your experience. You can't live a perfect life without making any messes.

The Bible uses agricultural language to say that to be productive you have to put up with a messy stall.

If the stall is empty, it remains clean. But where oxen are, there will be some mess (Prov. 14:4). Do you want to be productive or have a clean stall?

If you decide to get married and have children, I can guarantee you that you will experience some messes. It is inevitable that children will mess up the stall. That comes with the blessing of family. Children come complete with a problem quotient. Your option is to live by yourself and enjoy a less complicated life, or to accept the problems that come with having a family—along with the joys.

The key to living the fearless life is to be willing to take risks. That can be scary sometimes. Even when you choose to live the fearless life, you will sometimes feel afraid. The psalmist declared, "Whenever I am afraid, I will trust in You" (Ps. 56:3). Facing that fear is how you overcome fear of failure and live a happy, productive, fearless life.

COURAGEOUSNESS IS FEARLESSNESS

When my dad died suddenly at age fifty-six, he left behind a congregation that had looked to him as their Moses. I knew that fear had paralyzed them and was keeping them from their destiny as a church. After his funeral, God gave me a message for that church that would help them move ahead into their promised land.

I preached about Joshua's encounter with God after Moses's death. God told Joshua four times not to be afraid. And He gave him four reasons for not giving into fear. God knew the biggest enemy Joshua would face would not be the giants in the land—it would be the little voices inside telling him he could not do it. It would be the voices of fear screaming, "Who do you think you are? You are not able."

Are you facing a hard situation? Have your circumstances changed unexpectedly? You have to be willing to face down those frightening voices and take a risk to move forward into your destiny. You cannot give in to the spirit of timidity and draw back when times get tough.

God was giving Joshua a pep talk about the fearless life. He could have told Joshua how to assemble a great army and how to be a great leader. But the one thing He told him was not to allow a spirit of fear to get inside of him. If a spirit of fear begins to dominate you, it will make you draw back from the victory God has for you.

God has all power to work through you when you refuse fear. You have to face the giants. Then

God will fight for you and win the battle. God is saying to you what He said to Joshua. If you will be bold to obey whatever He tells you to do, you will continue to win! If you can stay free from the spirit of fear, nothing can defeat you. That's the fearless life.

Let's take a look at the reasons Joshua needed to be courageous in the face of fear.

Reason 1: Courage for the people's sake

First, God told Joshua to be strong and very courageous for the people's sake (Josh. 1:6). When you face life with courage and follow God with all your heart, there are others around you who will benefit from your success. Your family, friends, and others whom you influence will be able to follow you into the promised land because of your witness, your godly decisions, and your courage to take risks and live the fearless life.

Your life is not just about reaching your promised land and fulfilling your destiny. No one lives life in isolation. Your marriage, your children, your employer or employees, friends, and even lost souls around you are all watching you. They want to see if you will face trouble with courage or will buckle before it in fear. They can learn from you how to overcome fear as they see you courageously face obstacles to your success.

God spoke this reality to my heart in one of the darkest valleys I ever walked as a pastor. There was a battle raging against my ministry and the church. Mental, emotional, and physical fatigue overwhelmed me. There seemed to be little possible victory or reward in the face of overwhelming odds.

The Lord said to me, "Fear not, for the people's sake." His Word helped me to summon supernatural courage not to give up for their sake. And today God has won that overwhelming battle and given us a harvest of souls many times greater than I could have imagined. Every time faith is tested and courage prevails, it grows stronger and is equipped for greater victories to come.

Because the children of Israel crossed over into their Promised Land centuries ago, we are able to enter our promised land in Christ. They are part of our history as God's plan to bring forth the Messiah through that nation. We needed for them to succeed in order to fulfill God's plan for a Savior.

In that same way, there are people attached to your life, and God needs you to succeed because they are depending on you. You are not just learning to become fearless because of what you get out of it. God has attached others to your dream and destiny. Don't underestimate the power your life will have on future generations when you overcome fear for the people's sake.

Reason 2: Courage for your sake

God told Joshua to be fearless for his own sake. He told Joshua not to be afraid so that he could prosper everywhere he went (Josh 1:7). Joshua had been prepared in the wilderness and mentored by Moses to take Israel into the Promised Land. God did not want the fear of failure to paralyze Joshua from being able to accomplish the tremendous task that lay before him.

Are you cringing before an opportunity that seems too big for you? If you have committed your life to Christ, you can expect Him to give you the ability and resources you need to succeed. Your main goal is to resist fear and trust God to take you through that door of opportunity.

God had a lot invested in Joshua. The success or failure of an entire nation rested on his shoulders. He reminded Joshua to be fearless not only for the people's sake but also for his own sake, so that he would be prosperous wherever he went.

God has invested a lot in you too. As His child, you need to trust Him to give you good success for your sake. It is God's desire to prosper you in all you do.

Reason 3: Courage for the Lord's sake

God told Joshua not to be afraid for the Lord's sake (Josh. 1:9). He promised Joshua that He was with him wherever he went. The Lord had a bigger stake in Israel's success than they did. His eternal plan to bring forth the Messiah depended on the success of Israel. God was going to do His part to make these slaves into a nation that served the true God.

Pagan nations all around had observed the supernatural plagues God brought to deliver His people from Egypt. If they failed now to conquer their Promised Land, their failure would bring reproach to His great name. God needed Joshua to exhibit great courage for the Lord's sake.

God's reputation is on the line when He makes you a promise. If you fail to inherit His promises through fear, your failure ultimately affects the great heart of God. He loves you and has ordained for you to walk in His ways and fulfill your destiny by trusting in His great love. And He has a plan for your success.

Reason 4: Courage for the enemies' sake

God told Joshua not to be afraid for the enemies' sake (Josh. 1:18). God knew there were enemies waiting for this people. He told Joshua to display strength and courage when facing them. He promised to be with him and fight for him. Joshua just needed to conquer fear for the enemies' sake.

For your enemies' sake, God wants to prove His victory in your life. King David wrote: "You prepare a table before me in the presence of my enemies; You anoint my head with oil; my cup runs over" (Ps. 23:5). God vindicates His servants when they refuse to fear their enemies.

Sometimes it is good to have enemies. An enemy can press you into victory where a friend cannot. Who would ever have heard of David without Goliath? Would you have known about Moses if there had been no Pharaoh oppressing God's people? And what would you know about Esther without Haman's evil plot against the Jews?

What is keeping you from your dream? Is there an enemy standing between you and its fulfillment? Dare to confront your enemy without fear or intimidation, and it will become an instrument in God's hand to press you into your destiny.

Your heavenly Father is more zealous to protect you from your enemies than you are to protect your children from the school bully. When you submit to His lordship, He takes responsibility to fight for you. Sometimes God will bless you just because the enemy has come against you. It's like He says, "I'm not going to let you fail because you have so many enemies." You don't ever have to be afraid.

When Absalom, David's son, committed treason and drove his father from his throne, a man named Shimei followed along. He cursed David continually and threw stones at him. David's servant asked permission to kill Shimei. But David said, "Let him alone, and let him curse.... It may be that the LORD will look on my affliction, and that the LORD will repay me with good for his cursing this day" (2 Sam. 16:11–12). Absalom died that day, and the throne was restored to David. Once again God prepared a table for David in the presence of his enemies.

My dad's congregation was encouraged by this message to live fearlessly. That church became a larger, more powerful church than ever before. They did not draw back in fear. They went forward in the courage that God gave them to walk in their destiny.

WILL YOU FIGHT FOR YOUR "BEAN PATCH"?

King David showed his wisdom by surrounding himself with men of character and integrity. They were fearless men who were willing to die for their convictions. One of those men was named Shammah. He took a stand by himself in a field of lentils and fought the Philistines when everyone else ran away. He was devoted to David and fought alone against great odds to defend a patch of beans.

Why would a man be willing to die for a bean patch? Surely it was not because of the monetary value of those lentils. That ordinary bean patch was not precious; it was pivotal. Shammah understood that if he compromised that position, the enemy would keep coming and take more territory for themselves.

If he gave up the field, what would be next? His home? His children? His city? There is a powerful lesson in standing alone against fear. The moment you compromise one inch to fear, you will have to compromise more territory. And before you know it, you will lose everything you ever had in God because you did not take a stand.

What convictions have you compromised? Maybe it seems like a small thing—a glance at a pornographic magazine or website, using an expletive at work, cheating on your taxes. Understand that those seemingly small compromises are pivotal to your Christian life. When you give up little convictions in your life—little acts of obedience that no one notices—it becomes easier to compromise with bigger issues of life.

As Shammah defended that field, killing the Philistine enemies, God brought about a great victory. That death-defying battle became an opportunity for Shammah. He did not merely defeat the enemy that day; he also walked into his destiny to become one of David's mighty men.

You need to be like Shammah. Station yourself to fight the enemy alone when others flee. Stand firm for your smallest convictions even when others compromise with the enemy. That's how you aid the forces of righteousness in the unseen battle that God fights for you.

The only thing that keeps evil forces from fulfilling their assignments in you and your family is to put your foot down and say, "I may look like a fool, but this bean patch matters!" Your convictions matter!

Don't let any place of fear lodge in your heart without taking a stand against it. Do it just because it is right. Live in the principles of freedom and truth, and you will make a greater impact on others' lives than you ever dreamed possible. Nothing is too small to defend against the enemy's attack.

You Don't Have to Fear the Lion

One of my favorite Bible heroes is a man named Benaiah, who did not turn his back on danger. In fact, he pursued a lion, which is one of the most dangerous animals you can ever encounter. Known as the king of beasts because of their great strength, male lions can measure more than eight feet in length, not counting the tail.

These flesh eaters have thirty sharp, piercing teeth, canines to grab and kill prey and scissorlike molars to slice into flesh. And they are capable of high speed for short distances, especially when attacking fleet-footed prey.[10]

Benaiah was the son of a valiant warrior, Jehoiada (2 Sam. 23:20). It seems that the courage of his father had influenced Benaiah to become a fearless warrior also. On a snowy day Benaiah decided to pursue a lion, knowing that he would have to kill it or be killed in the encounter.

The Bible tells us the outcome of that encounter but not the details. It says that Benaiah jumped into a pit where the lion was and killed it. He was tracking the lion; the lion was not stalking him. Evidently he was alone. He had to rely on his courage to deliver him from a terrible death such as only a lion can inflict.

To live a fearless life you can't just be an average joe. You have to have the courage to take risks against all odds. You have to be like Benaiah and pursue the lion that poses a threat to you and your family.

That lion was an opportunity for Benaiah. Did he know that conquering that lion would become a part of his résumé? That it would open a door for his becoming one of David's mighty men? Probably not. Yet he pursued it just the same.

And after becoming King David's bodyguard, Benaiah was later promoted to be the captain of the host of all of Israel under King Solomon. He became the second most powerful man in Israel because of the fearless courage he displayed. Each dangerous situation Benaiah faced was God's opportunity for him to become fearless.

If you're going to be fearless, you must take advantage of opportunities. Don't wait to be attacked; go on the offensive when opportunity presents itself. God wants you to take advantage of your opportunities. If you sing, join the choir. If you are thinking about starting a new business, take the steps to investigate your possibilities. If you are lonely, make the effort to develop friendships.

It may seem like your scariest moment. I understand how you feel. But God loves to see you move out in faith and conquer your fears. When I said yes to that first opportunity to preach in my brother's revival service, I walked into that pulpit feeling scared and feeble.

I didn't know then that my fragile flapping wings were changing the spiritual weather patterns of my life. And I didn't dream that one little sermon would begin to blow change to the lives of a church in Gainesville, Georgia; to another church in Orange County, California; and to the nations of the world.

Look for and embrace the smallest opportunities God gives you. Pray and ask God to speak to you and show you what He wants you to do. When God is with you, He changes the odds. When God is in the equation, your nothingness plus God's almightiness equals more than enough.

Declare His Word: "I can do all things through Christ who strengthens me" (Phil. 4:13). Then, even if all you have is a maybe, you will be able to conquer your fear to step out in faith on that alone.

What to Do When All You Have Is a Maybe

Do you like to have a sure thing before you take a risk? Do you want to invest your money in something that guarantees a certain rate of return? Do you have to know that someone likes you before offering your friendship? Many times when God wants you to do something, it does not seem like a sure thing at first. Most of the great miracles in the Bible happened when people stepped out in faith on a maybe.

On one occasion Jonathan, the son of King Saul, was pursuing the great Philistine army. I was struck by what he said to his armor bearer. He did not say he had a word from the Lord and he knew they were going to win the battle. Jonathan simply said to him,

"Come, let us go over to the garrison of these uncircumcised; it *may be* that the LORD will work for us" (1 Sam. 14:6, emphasis added). Maybe the Lord will help them? And if He didn't, what then? Doesn't sound like a risk-free proposition.

Jonathan had faith that God was with him. He thought He might fight with him against these enemies of Israel. Still, he was not sure what would happen in that confrontation. So he said, "It may be…" Jonathan and his armor bearer risked their lives in faith with just a maybe.

As they showed themselves to the Philistines, they began to fight a few of them in an open field, slaughtering about twenty men. The Lord was with Jonathan and caused the entire Philistine army to erupt in great confusion. The Philistines began to kill each other and to flee before these two warriors who had dared to trust God with their maybe.

The trap of waiting for a sure thing

Always remember that fearlessness is not the absence of fear; it's the mastery of fear. You have to master the fear of uncertainty. King Solomon, the wisest man who ever lived, said, "He who observes the wind will not sow, and he who regards the clouds will not reap" (Eccles. 11:4).

Solomon was saying that you have to take a chance sometimes even when it seems the weather is against you. Otherwise you will never do anything worthwhile. It is better to sow seed and reap the harvest in spite of contrary winds and other uncertainties.

If you are like me, you want to wait to take a risk until conditions are perfect and you are absolutely sure that you will succeed. You want to know what the clouds are going to do and the effect of the wind on your endeavor.

I don't always have a sermon that I am absolutely certain is the word of the Lord for that

> Always remember that fearlessness is not the absence of fear; it's the mastery of fear.

moment every time I step into the pulpit to preach. Sometimes I'm iffy about what the Lord wants me to preach. Many times when I have preached the iffy message I had prepared, the Lord has worked mightily in the hearts and lives of believers and unbelievers alike.

It would be wonderful if God would send you a text message from heaven or an angel to thump you on the head to give you divine direction. More often, God speaks in a still, small voice or an impression that you receive in prayer or when reading the Word. He might give you an idea when you are listening to someone preach or are reading the newspaper. That idea or impression begins to grow inside, and you wonder if it could be God—maybe He wants you to do this.

We like the guaranteed outcome. We are comfortable with the certain, absolute deal, with no risk of failure or loss. But the truth is, we are going to face a maybe more times than we will have guarantees. It is those times of uncertainty that try our resolve, prove our faith, and test our courage.

Your faith and courage are strengthened more readily when you explore a maybe as you meditate on His Word and submit yourself to the lordship of Christ. You may not be comfortable with this level of dependency on God. Your mind and carnal desire are to have the clear understanding of a sure thing. But faith in God's maybe is a safe place. God can turn that maybe into a miracle.

I am not talking about being presumptuous or pressing for your own personal desires. Sometimes when we want something to happen, we presume that God does too. When you feel like God is saying something to you, especially if it involves a major decision, you should seek the counsel of your pastor or other spiritual leaders in your life.

I never make a major decision in life without allowing two or three spiritual leaders to confirm it. That is a biblical principle for seeking godly counsel. I ask them to pray about it and see if God tells them something contrary.

After seeking counsel, ask yourself: "Is my motive right? Do I want only to do God's will?" Then you can say with confidence: "It may be the Lord is with me."

I have watched God work miracles for me many times when I was willing to seek Him and move out in faith on a maybe. My motive was right; I was praying and studying and waiting on God. I sought counsel and then moved

> Faith in God's maybe is a safe place. God can turn that maybe into a miracle.

in faith against all odds. And God transformed my maybe into a miracle.

The secret to tapping into the supernatural is for you to have the courage to do the natural first. Jonathan knew he was no match for the Philistine army, but he courageously faced them with a maybe that the Lord would be with him. Without his action, God could not change his maybe into a miracle.

What are your options?

Consider your options. If you are in a financial struggle, will you cave in to fear and let failure win? Will you let your dream for starting a business die inside you because of the risk involved? Is that potential relationship too scary to pursue? Will you compromise your godly convictions to please your children?

Don't wait for guarantees. Don't sit still and do nothing because your actions may carry a risk. Don't fear natural circumstances, obstacles, or frightening situations. Take the maybe you have been given, and begin to act on it. You will begin to see the hand of God turn it into a miracle if you refuse to give in to fear.

If you are willing to face off with the fear of failure that has held you back from fulfilling your divine destiny, I encourage you to pray this prayer with me:

> *Dear Lord Jesus, help me to define failure and success as You do and not as the world does. Let me pursue the success*

You have ordained for my sake, for the sake of others, for Your sake, and for the enemy's sake. Let me have strength to step out on a maybe that You give me and pursue the lion that threatens my dream. Help me not to compromise my smallest convictions. Thank You for setting me free from the fear of failure. Let me grow in faith and benefit from times when I fail. And let me experience Your miracle in my maybe situation. Amen.

3

FEARLESS ABOUT PEOPLE

GOD CALLED JEREMIAH as a young man to be a prophet. Jeremiah protested that he was young and could not speak. Then God told him that he would go wherever He sent him and speak whatever He told him to speak. And God said, "Do not be afraid of their faces, for I am with you to deliver you" (Jer. 1:8). He addressed Jeremiah's fear of people and promised to deliver him.

I wonder how many potential relationships have been thwarted because of a fear of people. This learned fear is one of the most detrimental to building marriages, friendships, and strong relationships. I shared with you how timid I was when I was a young man. Unless God had helped me to overcome my fear, I would not have enjoyed the wonderful marriage I have or many other vital relationships that have impacted my life.

If relationships of any kind spark anxiety and fear in your heart, I have good news for you. Jesus wants to set you free to experience meaningful relationships. There is no rejection in His love, only complete acceptance. There is no condemnation, just forgiveness and mercy.

Jesus wanted people to know the love of God, so He taught them the great value that He puts on every individual life. As usual, He started His teaching by asking them about something they were very familiar with—roasted sparrows.

In those days, vendors carried on commerce in the open market by setting up small booths along the streets. Some vendors sold sparrows on a stick that they had roasted over an open fire. (They did not have McDonald's in those days; they had McSparrow's.)

Jesus said you could buy two of those roasted sparrows for one copper coin. But in some places, according to Jesus, you could get five sparrows for two copper coins. Obviously, shrewd vendors threw in a fifth sparrow for free.

Third-grade math tells you that if two sparrows

are sold for one copper coin, you should be able to buy four sparrows for two copper coins. But Jesus knew you could buy five sparrows for two small coins. That meant the fifth sparrow was worthless. It really had no value for the vendor. That fifth sparrow could be called the odd bird out. It's similar to our expression of someone being "a fifth wheel."

Then Jesus told the people that not one sparrow falls to the ground without God noticing it. That would include even the worthless fifth sparrow. And Jesus said, "Do not fear therefore; you are of more value than many sparrows" (Luke 12:7).

WHEN YOU FEEL "LESS THAN"

Jesus wanted them to be convinced that they did not have to be afraid; they were safe in God's love. He is saying the same to you today. Have you ever felt as worthless as that fifth sparrow? In tough times life can tell you that you are nobody, headed nowhere. But Jesus does not want anyone to feel like a fifth sparrow. You are of great worth to God.

Regardless of what life has dealt to you that makes you feel less than, God still says you matter to Him. He sees great value in you. If you can believe that, you will have the power to conquer the fear of rejection. When you know how valuable you are to God, you will not fear what others think of you.

Jesus urged us over and over in Scripture to observe the fowl of the air. He wants us to learn valuable spiritual lessons from the birds. But not just any birds; He mentioned sparrows specifically. He focused on these little birds that even today are considered common and insignificant among the bird community.

He didn't say to observe the strutting peacock. I learned a long time ago that today's strutting peacock can become tomorrow's feather duster. You need to be careful when you start strutting around in pride because of the blessing of God.

Don't ever forget where you came from. Remember what life was like before you knew Christ. And stay humble before the Lord in gratitude for what He has given you. The Lord values your humility and loathes your pride.

Jesus didn't specifically mention the beautiful cardinal, the noisy blue jay, or any other exotic bird we consider more valuable. He asked us to think about the common little sparrow. He told the people that little bird mattered to God. And He also told them they were of much more value than many sparrows.

God says that to you also. Do you know how valuable you are to God? He created you in His image. His whole purpose was for you to live in perfect fellowship with Him, not only in this life but also forever. And through Christ's death on Calvary He bought you back to Himself to enjoy that communion with Him.

There are no fifth sparrows in God's mind. In fact, He is aware of every one of those little birds that falls to the ground. How much more is He aware of you? God says that even though people may not see value in you, He does. You are very valuable to Him.

Did you catch what Jesus said about those sparrows falling to the ground? God attends their funerals. I have never been to a sparrow's funeral, but He never misses one. God's great loving heart cares even for a sparrow that falls.

He knows what makes you feel worthless. When you wonder if you have any value or contribution to make to life, when you are falling to the ground in a quiet despair of worthlessness, God is there. You may think no one even knows you exist. But if God goes to the funeral of a fallen sparrow, He knows and cares about you, even when you mess up.

God specializes in restoring "fallen ones." Jesus's message about the sparrow is for you if you were soaring at one time in life but something happened and you failed. Or someone devastated your self-worth, making you feel rejected. You became afraid and began to feel like a fifth sparrow or fifth wheel, like you don't fit; you are the odd bird out without value or worth.

God wants you to know that if He cares about a fallen sparrow, He certainly cares about you when you fall and mess up. You are of great value in God's equation of love and grace! In short, there are no fifth sparrows with God—every person has great value in God's perspective. You count with Him. You are somebody to Him. And even when people don't put any worth in you anymore, God will never give up on you.

Self-exaltation leads to pride, which God hates. But self-deprecation leads to paralysis. It creates a terrible atmosphere where fear prevails. Neither attitude is pleasing to God. The devil has made a lot of people feel as if they are not worth anything—that they are just a big failure, and their lives are one big mistake after another.

If you believe his lie, you let life paint you into the picture of a fifth sparrow that is worthless, that doesn't fit in. Other people have value; they succeed. But whatever has happened in your life makes you feel as though you are less than other people.

You need to know that Jesus displayed your great value to Him when He hung on a cross at Calvary. He loved you personally so much that He was willing to lay down His life for you so that you could be free to be the person He made you to be. And He told you not to be afraid that you have failed God so much that He doesn't love you anymore.

I don't care how many times you have tried and failed. God's message to you is that He still loves you. The smallest detail of your life does not escape God's gaze. He still sees worth in you. He knows your potential. And He has a plan and purpose for

> Self-exaltation leads to pride, which God hates. But self-deprecation leads to paralysis. It creates a terrible atmosphere where fear prevails. Neither attitude is pleasing to God.

your life. His love for you is special. It's like God has your picture on His refrigerator.

WHEN YOU FEEL LIKE AN OUTSIDER

I think everyone faces the feeling at some time of being the odd bird out, of standing alone without the approval of others. You may be in a season of feeling like you are not as special or valuable as other members of your family or your friends—or even of your brothers and sisters in Christ. There were people in the Bible who were considered odd birds by others. The Bible tells us how God thinks about them.

David was the odd bird. He was treated like the fifth sparrow of the family. Do you remember when Samuel was sent to the house of Jesse, David's father, to anoint the next king of Israel? They had a big banquet, and then it came time to anoint one of his seven sons who were present. Samuel looked at each one and admired them for their physical appearance.

Their father would recommend each one to Samuel as they passed before him. "This boy is handsome. This boy has real talent. This one is very intelligent. I think this one would make an excellent king!"

But God spoke to Samuel that He had refused all of these sons. He told him that He does not see as man sees; man looks at the outward appearance, but He looks at the heart (1 Sam. 16:7). So Samuel asked Jesse if he had any other sons.

Jesse said his youngest son was in the field keeping the sheep. His daddy had not even invited him to the feast. He was just the youngest son, not yet worth much to his family. His father did not even consider presenting him to the prophet. He was like the fifth sparrow that did not have any value among his peers.

I have learned something about God. He often passes over the hotshots and picks from the back of the line. God loves to choose people whom others pass over, reject, and put down. They predict, "He or she will never amount to anything."

But if you let God put His hand on you, He will choose you over the hotshots. He looks at your heart and says, "I can use him. I can use her." When you humble yourself under the mighty hand of God, He will exalt you in due time (1 Pet. 5:6). Don't let anyone tell you that you are a fifth sparrow!

WHEN YOU FACE ALONENESS AND LONELINESS

The psalmist expressed feelings of aloneness and dejection when he said, "I am like a pelican of the wilderness; I am like an owl of the desert...and am like a sparrow alone on the housetop" (Ps. 102:6–7). He felt like an odd bird, alone.

Even Jesus knew what it meant to be alone without people who understood Him. His disciples did not understand Him. They were concerned about which of them was the greatest. They could not even pray with Him in His most difficult moments. And on the cross He cried out, "My God, my God, why hast thou forsaken me?" (Matt. 27:46, KJV).

Aloneness can do a number on your sense of worth. Some of you—because of the rejection of a friend, a divorce, the death of a loved one, or other painful circumstances— are walking through a season where you feel like the odd bird. You don't have anyone who really understands what you are going through. Life has dealt you a blow that has made you feel less than.

> Even Jesus knew what it meant to be alone without people who understood Him. His disciples did not understand Him.

I remember a time when my wife and I took a cruise and we noticed people who sat alone during the entire cruise. They ate every meal alone. And our hearts were touched by their aloneness. But I also know that there are times when you can be in a crowd and still feel lonely.

Everyone faces times of aloneness and loneliness. The good news is that even if your earthly relationships are in trouble, the Lord wants you to know that He will never leave you alone or forsake you (Heb. 13:5). He will be there for you. He will never abandon you. You don't have to be afraid of being alone. He will show you the way out of your pain and loneliness.

I understand the fear that grips people who wonder if they will ever find the right person to marry. For every person who has a desire for marriage, I believe you can trust God that your perfect mate is living and breathing somewhere on the planet. God has the greatest dating service in the world. It is better than "Find-a-Mate.com." If you will seek God first and decide to serve Him with all your heart, He will move heaven and earth to cross your paths with that special person.

Whether you are widowed, divorced, or have

never married, don't be anxious. God is in control of your love life if you submit your life to Him. Your steps are ordered of the Lord. It is exciting to watch the future unfold when you place your confidence in His goodness and His plan for your life. God has opportunities for you that you have never dreamed possible.

My mother's story

My dad had a heart attack and died suddenly at the age of fifty-six. My mother was a young widow, left alone with my sixteen-year-old sister, Jill. The small inheritance Dad had left lasted only a couple of years. Then they began to experience financial need. All my mom had ever known was the life of a minister's wife and homemaker.

She is not the type of person who would talk about her situation to anyone, not even to my brothers and sisters or me. Instead, she determined to seek the Lord in fasting and prayer. She committed to pray and fast for three days as Queen Esther of old had done.

Mom had no idea what she was going to do to make it through those tough times. One day during her fast she prayed, "Lord, if You will direct my steps, I will go anywhere and do whatever You want me to do. I will work a secular job and witness for You by my lifestyle. I will take a position in a church or ministry. As long as I know You are leading me, I will do whatever You want me to do."

When she finished praying that prayer, she laid her head down to rest. Not five minutes later, her telephone rang. When she answered the phone, she heard the voice of my wife, Cherise. My wife didn't greet her in a normal way with "hello" or any small talk. She came straight to the point and said, "Well, you might as well pack your things because you're coming. Here's Jentezen."

Of course, I had no clue that Mom had been praying about direction for her life; all I knew was that I needed help. I got on the phone and said, "Mom, I've been asking you for two years to come and help me. The church is growing so fast that I don't have time to pray and study like I should while I'm just trying to keep up with everything. I need you to help me with hospital visits and to love the people. I need you to do for me what you did for Daddy's ministry. If you don't come, I'm going to hire someone else, so I need you to tell me now if you're coming."

My mom began to give me all kinds of excuses.

Her life had been wrapped up in my dad's ministry, and she still had trouble making decisions sometimes. She never had to make a big decision like this one on her own. While she continued with her excuses, the Lord reminded her of what she had just prayed minutes earlier: "I will do whatever You want me to do."

Mom finally said yes, and on September 2, 1993, she moved to Gainesville, Georgia, to become a part of my staff at Free Chapel. Now, years later, Mom is one of the most loved and active members of my staff. She and her loyal volunteers visit rest homes each week. They bring those precious people a message of hope and brighten their day with music.

Mom also leads our convalescent care ministry, which offers wonderful home-cooked meals to comfort families who have lost loved ones.

Whenever our members have a serious need and call the church for prayer, they don't ask for me; they ask for my mom. She is absolutely vital to the ministry, and our entire congregation values her immensely. She dared to leave her home and all that was familiar to become a part of the ministry at Free Chapel. Her loving surrender to obedience to the Lord opened for her an amazing opportunity for life-giving ministry.

God knows your aloneness just as He knew my mother's. He knows that you can be extremely useful and fruitful in His kingdom if you will determine to overcome your fear and seek Him for His divine opportunities.

JESUS SEEKS OUT THE LONELY

Jesus typically sought out the people who were alone in a crowd. He called His disciples individually to follow Him. And He had an appointment with a solitary Samaritan woman who came to a well to draw water. He offered her living water that changed her life. He offered the man at the pool of Bethesda the cure he could not receive otherwise, because he had no one to help him get into the water.

After His resurrection Jesus did not go to Rome or Athens or any other metropolis. There is no record that He visited the multitudes. He revealed Himself to a lonely, grief-stricken woman outside the tomb. When He called her name, "Mary," she knew His voice. He walked with two troubled men on the road to Emmaus, and they recognized Him when He broke bread with them. And He appeared to His disciples hiding in fear behind closed doors.

Jesus was constantly reaching out to the down-and-outers, the lonely, the odd birds. If that is how you feel, then you can expect to have a special audience with the Lord. He wants to spend time with you to tell you that you don't have to be afraid of aloneness.

You are not alone when Christ is with you. He does not consider you a fifth sparrow. He sees you when you fall. Why? Because He cares about every detail of your life.

> Jesus was constantly reaching out to the down-and-outers, the lonely, the odd birds. If that is how you feel, then you can expect to have a special audience with the Lord.

God has a plan for your life, and He wants you to walk with Him to fulfill it—together. His promise to you is this: "For I know the thoughts that I think toward you, says the LORD, thoughts of peace and not of evil, to give you a future and a hope" (Jer. 29:11).

No matter how great your failure, He has a plan for your life filled with hope and not despair. I dare you to declare, "God only thinks good things about me and plans good things for me." It is true, because He loves you with an everlasting love—a love that made Him lay down His life for you. He will never reject you or leave you alone. In that reality you can have hope to overcome those fears. The psalmist declared that God's thoughts toward him were precious and were so many that he could not count them (Ps. 139:17–18).

You have a home in God, in His heart, and in His thoughts. There is a place even for the insignificant sparrow to dwell in the presence of God. The psalmist said that the sparrow had found a house for herself where she could raise her young in the altars of God (Ps. 84:3).

He allowed the most insignificant fifth sparrow to dwell in His presence. She was safe to build her nest and raise her family in that place of worship, the holy tabernacle. That is a beautiful picture of your safe place in the presence of God. As you bow in worship, He will lift you up and make you feel valuable and safe. He will deliver you from the fear of rejection and aloneness.

You can't hide *from* God, but you can hide *in* God. You can nest in His safety and in His protection, blessing, and presence. You can never feel alone or afraid in His presence. No matter what life throws your way, you don't have to feel like you are less than. You are important to God. His love will always be there for you even in seasons of trouble and loss.

WHEN EVERYONE TURNS AGAINST YOU

I thought about Job, who was one of the wealthiest men of his time. The Bible says he feared God and hated evil. Yet in one day the bottom dropped out of his life. He lost his wealth, his children, and his health, and he was betrayed by his wife. She told him to curse God and die. Then four of his friends came and sat around him as he sat on the ash heap.

For seven days they just sat there, not saying a word, just looking at him with an accusing look. He sat there, the fifth sparrow in the middle of those four friends. They were there to tell him how he had failed God. They wanted him to confess the sin that had caused all this calamity. They accused him of messing up. Their long speeches told him all the reasons they knew he was not the righteous man he claimed to be.

What did Job do? He had to decide how he was going to face his adversity. He could not deny the bad news. Everything that he valued in life had been lost. But he settled it in his heart. He would not accuse God or feel sorry for himself. He simply declared, "The LORD gave, and the LORD hath taken away; blessed be the name of the LORD" (Job 1:21, KJV). He knew the greatest thing in life was the presence of the Lord. Job chose to bless the name of the Lord in his painful aloneness.

When his wife told him to curse God and die, Job said, "No, thank you. I will bless the name of the Lord and live! I still have His presence! I don't understand why all this is happening, but I know that He is with me." And the Bible says that God restored to Job twice as much as he had in the beginning.

What have you lost? Are you tempted to blame God for your painful situation? I encourage you to do as Job did and bless the name of the Lord. He is with you in your pain, and He can turn your weeping into joy once again. He wants to give you a safe place to dwell in His presence continually. You are not alone. You don't have to be afraid in your adversity.

MASTER OR MASCOT?

It became obvious to all that God was truly Job's Master. In the cruelest adversity Job honored Him as his God. He chose to bless the name of the Lord. That is the key to overcoming any fear.

God takes what the world says is worthless and reveals the great value He has placed in you. But He demands to be Master and Lord of your life. That is His rightful place. A lot of people want God to take their sin and guilt and let them enjoy their freedom. But then they treat Him as their mascot and not their Master.

Do you know what a mascot is? It's like the University of Georgia's bulldog. During halftime of a football game, that bulldog is taken out of his crate, and he runs across the field. Everybody hoops and hollers for their mascot. Then he is put back in the crate and taken back to his kennel until next week's game.

That's what a lot of Christians do with Jesus. They come to church one day a week and get excited in the presence of the Lord. Then they live the rest of the week without thinking about Him. And Jesus says, "You don't talk to Me. You don't listen to Me. You don't read My Word. I want to be Master on

Monday, Tuesday, Wednesday, Thursday, Friday, and Saturday. I'm not a mascot to applaud on Sunday. I am your Master. And if you will give Me your life, I will do something with it!"

The devil wants you to feel like a fifth sparrow—worthless, odd, and insignificant. God wants to make your life significant. He wants to develop all the potential He placed inside of you to contribute to His purposes in the earth. You will not feel insignificant if you will make Him Lord and Master of your life.

WHEN YOU'RE ASHAMED

I love this true story about an odd bird who came to know God as His Master. A seminary professor and his family were vacationing in the hills of Tennessee. They stopped in a little country town in East Tennessee to eat a meal in a local diner there. When they were seated, they ordered their meal.

As they were served, they noticed an old man going from table to table talking to the customers. The professor cringed at the thought that the man might come to their table. He wished he would just leave them alone. But sooner than he would have liked, the old man came to talk to them.

"How ya'll doin?' he asked. Then without waiting for an answer: "Ya'll aren't from these parts, are ya?"

"No."

"Well, where ya'll from, and what do ya do?"

"We are from Oklahoma, and I am a seminary professor."

"Oh, really? So, you teach preachers how to preach, do ya? Ya know, I once knew a pastor who impacted my life in such a way that it changed me forever." The old man was gaining interest in his recollection.

"How do you mean?" asked the professor, trying to be polite as he took another bite of his meal.

"Well, I've grown up in these parts of East Tennessee all my life. This is a very small community. Everybody knows everybody and everybody's business. So, everybody knows I never knew who my father was. I was illegitimate. Everywhere I went, it seemed someone was taunting me with the question, 'Who's your daddy?'"

He continued, thoughtfully, "All my life I felt less than others, you know. I felt odd. When I played ball, all the other kids had a dad at the game. All I ever had was my mother and grandmother. And somehow I felt ashamed. In public, I sat in the corner. I isolated myself from others. I felt inferior because I did not have a father."

The old man's eyes glistened as he said, "Then, one day, my grandmother started taking me to church. I will never forget it. I started listening to what that preacher was sayin.' And one Sunday, when we was leavin,' the preacher was at the door shaking hands with the people. As I went by, he shook my hand. Then he bent over and whispered something in my ear."

Now, the old man was wiping tears, unashamed, before he went on with his story. "He whispered in my ear, 'Son, I know who your father is. Your father is God. And He's the best Father that any person could ever have. And don't you let anyone tell you any different.'"

Then the old man looked the professor right in the eye and said, "I can't explain it, but something clicked inside of me that day. A light came on. I began to see God as my own Father. And you know what? God has been very good to me."

With that, the old man left their table and walked out of the diner. When the professor and his family finished eating, he went to the cash register and asked, "You know that old man who was walking around talking to everyone?"

"Yeah."

"Well, who is he? And what is his deal?" queried the professor, trying to hide his sarcasm.

"You don't know?" asked the man behind the cash register, incredulously. "Why, that is Ben Hooper. He is the former two-term governor of Tennessee [1910–1914)]. And he has done more good for this community and this entire state than anyone I know. He is an amazing man!"[1]

That's what can happen when you realize that you are not a fifth sparrow. You don't have to live in shame because of what your mother or father did— or because of what you have done. Somebody had to tell Ben Hooper that he was of great value to God, that God was his heavenly Father. Ben had to know that just because he was taunted as an illegitimate son, it didn't mean that he had no value. In fact, the

Bible says that God is a "father of the fatherless" (Ps. 68:5).

The psalmist said, "When my father and my mother forsake me, then the LORD will take care of me" (Ps. 27:10). If God allowed you to be separated from your biological father, perhaps He knew that you would not have connected with His plan otherwise. If you make Christ the Master of your life, you can know the same kind of loving care that Ben Hooper discovered.

Ben Hooper's pastor knew that day that he was talking to a hurting little boy who needed to know who his father was. He needed to know that God was the best Father anyone could have. God showed Ben Hooper how much He loved him, how valuable and special he was. He was not a fifth sparrow. He was of great worth to his Father. And, in turn, he was able to bless thousands of lives by becoming all God meant for him to be.

You don't have to fear aloneness, because you are never alone. And you don't have to fear relationships, because God gives grace to love others and to forgive. He teaches you how to show mercy and to enjoy the love and fellowship He provides.

Some of you feel like the fifth sparrow sold on

that skewer for pennies. Life has stuck it to you and roasted you. You feel worthless in life. That is a lie from the devil. God does not have any fifth sparrows in His economy. He loves you, and He has a plan for your life. God has a place for you and a purpose that will bring fulfillment and satisfaction to your life.

You simply have to answer this question, "Is He Master or mascot? Does He sit on the throne of your heart?" When that issue is settled, you will begin to know His love and be set free from fear of loneliness, rejection, and all of the other fears related to relationships with others.

Jesus built a whole doctrine on the eradication of fear based on the value of one sparrow (Luke 12:7). If you want to ask God to set you free from these fears, pray this prayer with me:

> *Dear Lord Jesus, I come to make You Master of my life. I want to submit to Your lordship and find Your purpose for my life. I break the fear of rejection and aloneness over my life, in the name of Jesus. I declare that I am free from fear as a child of God. And I thank You,*

Lord, for Your power working in my life to give me a future and a hope. Thank You for the relationships You have for me. You will give me all I need in friends and family. I confess that I will not be alone, because You are with me. And Your love for me is setting me free from fear. Thank You, Jesus. I love You.

4

FEARLESS ABOUT HAVING ENOUGH

Recession. Foreclosure. Unemployment. Bankruptcy. Inflation. Fraud. Corruption. Exploding national deficit. Fiscal cliffs. These fear-laced words describe the economic condition of our world that is becoming more and more dependent on a global economy. Millions of people are not just hearing them; they are also living one or more of these dire financial scenarios.

It is a fact that our world continually faces difficult times of financial crisis. It is also a fact that you don't have to be afraid concerning your finances. The Word of God is still true. It says, "For God has not given you a spirit of fear, but of power and of love and of a sound mind" (2 Tim. 1:7). You don't have to be afraid of your financial situation, either present or future. Faith in God's Word during times of financial crisis will conquer all fear.

If local and national government, financial institutions, personal wealth, or productivity is your source of financial security, you may experience a terrible letdown. Your fear levels may rise to the point of causing serious physical and mental distress. It is time to evaluate your options. Do you know what the Word of God teaches about your financial provision? What promises does God give you to conquer your fear of financial ruin?

ATTACK YOUR LACK

Sometimes we are in financial difficulty because of our own poor choices or mistakes. At other times there are situations we didn't create that make our lives difficult. There are times we can feel like victims of other peoples' decisions, of an unexpected illness or accident, or of a worldwide economic crisis that threatens our financial future. The playing field is not always level when it comes to our financial security.

Disasters strike. The good news is that God is Master in times of disaster. Whether from your poor choices or from circumstances beyond your control, when you call on God, He will resolve your financial mess. Even if your financial distress is self-inflicted, God has a plan to get you out. You don't need to be tormented by fear about your finances.

I want to show you how to attack your lack. It starts with your mentality regarding finances. Some people have a poverty mentality. They may have been raised poor or for some reason expect to be poor all their lives. They just talk about their financial lack all the time.

> Disasters strike. The good news is that God is Master in times of disaster.

If you have this mentality, your first attack against your financial lack is to change your thinking.

There was a widow in the Old Testament who was destitute because of circumstances beyond her control (2 Kings 4:1). Her husband had died and left her with two sons and a pile of debt. Because of the debt, the creditor was coming to take her sons away to be his slaves. Desperate, she sent for the man of God, the prophet Elisha, and asked for his help.

Elisha asked her what she had in the house. She said she had nothing but a jar of oil. Then he told her to borrow as many empty vessels from all her neighbors as she could. She was to close the door and have her sons help her pour that little jar of oil into all those empty vessels.

When she obeyed the word of the prophet, the oil was multiplied and flowed until all the vessels were filled. Then he told her to go and sell the oil and pay her debt. There was enough left over for her family to live on the profit from that sale.

The playing field was not level for this widow. But when she called on God, He became the Master of her disaster. He has a plan for you if you will seek Him to release you from your financial disaster.

QUALIFYING FOR GOD'S ABUNDANCE

God told Abraham that He was going to bless him so that he could be a blessing to nations. Prosperity has been misunderstood by many preachers and teachers over the years. It's not about asking God to bless you for your own sake. Godly prosperity always has a purpose that is bigger than you; it is God's will to give you prosperity so that you in turn become a blessing to others.

Are you nervous or afraid about your financial situation? You need to remind yourself that God is your source of financial provision. Start declaring,

"It is God who insures my success this year. It is God who has the power to meet my needs. It is God who has the power to give me more than enough so that I can bless others in His name!"

Jesus told thirty-eight parables that deal with money management. There are five hundred verses about prayer and fasting, compared to two thousand on money and possessions from Jesus's teachings. That is five times more teaching on money than He did on prayer.

Why did Jesus teach more on money than He did on prayer? Why is money so important to Jesus? Because He knows that if you do not master money, it will master you.

You do not qualify for God's abundance until you first become His child. God loves to provide for His children even more than earthly fathers love to provide for their children. You have to decide to become a child of God through faith in His Son, Jesus Christ. Then all the promises of God become yours. I have five kids, and they can eat out of our refrigerator anytime. But if kids from the neighborhood came to raid our fridge, I would have a problem with that. They have their own parents who are to provide for them.

God wants to be your Father, and He wants His children to prosper—His way. The psalmist said that when you delight in God, everything you do will prosper (Ps. 1). You need to understand the generous heart of God for you to have abundance. He wants to change your poverty mentality. You have to believe His promises and confess that it is God's will for you to prosper. Your faith will set you free from fear of financial failure.

In the story of the prodigal son, the father is a picture of our heavenly Father. When that boy repented and came home, his father told his servants to kill the fatted calf, bring the best robe, give him shoes, and put a ring on his son's finger. That is the heart of our heavenly Father to bless His children with His best.

One key to the fearless life is the declaration of the psalmist that he was young and is now old and has not seen the righteous forsaken or his descendants begging for bread (Ps. 37:25). That divine promise is yours for you and your children to enjoy God's abundance when you live as a child of God. He has promised that no matter how old you get, He will take care of you. You will never be a beggar or a pauper. God will never forsake you when you qualify for His abundance.

When I went to India, I saw people starving in the streets. Cows mingled among the people. My mouth watered thinking of all that beefsteak running around. But they would not eat one of them because cows are considered to be gods. They worship the animal that God provided as food for their nourishment.

More than half of the grain produced in India is eaten by rats.[1] They don't kill them, because they are considered gods also. Because they do not serve the living God, they are doomed to poverty and starvation. How they need to know the wonderful news of the gospel that would set their captive hearts free!

I am so glad I worship the living God who wants me to prosper. He gave all things to us to enjoy in Christ. The difference between living in prosperity and living in poverty is a choice. Choices have consequences. God told Israel that He set death and life, blessing and cursing, before them. They had to choose life or death (Deut. 30:19). It is not by chance that you are blessed; it is by choice.

Giving is a choice. Jesus said if you give, it will

be given back to you according to the way that you give (Luke 6:38). Jesus taught that if you give, you will receive a "four-way gain clause": (1) good measure, (2) pressed down, (3) shaken together, and (4) running over.

Givers gain. Nothing multiplied by nothing is nothing. God multiplies seed that is sown. The Bible teaches that he who sows sparingly will also reap sparingly (2 Cor. 9:6). It is a law of harvest. Conversely, if you sow generously, you will reap generously. According to the way you sow, you will reap. This law of harvest applies to your finances as well. You will gain largely when you give largely, but you have to qualify by choosing to be a giver.

Diligence is a choice. The Bible says that we are to work six days and rest on the seventh day. There are two kinds of people God will not bless: lazy people and stingy people. You cannot be successful without hard work. God's Word does not teach an entitlement mentality that feels others owe you something. It teaches that a lazy person will live in need and have nothing, but the soul of the diligent will prosper (Prov. 13:4). It seems a little obvious, but I'll say it anyway: the first way to fight poverty is to get a job and do your job with diligence as working unto the Lord.

Sin is a choice. Sin brings poverty, low living, addictions, and destroyed lives. Living under a financial curse of sin is a choice. If you choose not to give, not to work, not to be responsible for the prosperity God wants to give to His children, you will bring a curse of poverty to your life.

RESPONSIBILITY OF STEWARDSHIP

God wants you to understand that money comes with responsibility. When Jesus taught the parable of the talents in Matthew 25, He was teaching about how to handle money. A talent was a sum of money, and Jesus told the story of a landowner who had great possessions, which he left in charge of his servants when he went on a long journey.

The landowner, a picture of God the Father, left His servants in charge of His goods. He gave five talents to one, two talents to another, and one talent to the last, according to their ability. They were responsible for the proper investment of his funds until he returned.

The first two servants used the money wisely and increased the landowner's investment. The third buried his one talent because he was afraid. When the landowner returned, he commended the first two servants for the increase of his talents. When the third servant offered the one talent back to the landowner, he was rebuked for not at least putting it in a bank to gain interest. The landowner called him wicked and slothful for his irresponsibility. Then he took the talent and gave it to the one who had used his five talents wisely.

The money did not belong to the servants; it belonged to the landowner. They were responsible for investing it wisely. You need to have the mentality that God is the rightful owner of everything He gives you. You are the manager to use His gifts responsibly. It's God's house that you live in. The clothes you wear are God's. It's God's money you spend. You don't own it, but as a steward you have rights to use it and must take responsibility for the way you do.

As you learn to practice the principles of God's Word regarding tithing and giving, the curse of lack will be broken over your life. His promise of prosperity is based on your obedience to His Word. When you seek His will and obey His commandments, you will walk in divine destiny and enjoy the prosperity God desires for you.

RELEASE TO INCREASE

God never intended for His children to be in slavery to debt permanently. You may be in a financial mess now, but God has a way out for you. Your slavery to financial loss, depression, fear, drugs, and alcohol is not a permanent state. He wants to release you to divine increase in every area of your life. Jesus came to set the captives free.

God has given promises to His children for prosperity and blessing since the earliest of times. He told Abraham that He would make him a great nation and multiply him in blessing so much that he would be a blessing to the nations. God's intention for His children is that they be blessed in every way.

If you are in a financial mess, you need to understand that your present is not your future. Your problem is temporary if you walk with God, because He intends to bless His children. God does not want you to give into a poverty mentality and think, "I will never get out of this." That is not God's voice. His voice is always a voice of freedom and hope.

The apostle Paul wrote the entire Book of Galatians to explain to us our inheritance of the promises of Abraham through Jesus Christ. As Christians, we are in the bloodline of blessing through the blood of Christ. Those blessings include financial freedom from economic slavery.

One of the great Hebrew names for God is Jehovah-Jireh, our provider. He is able to deliver you from every yoke of bondage to debt, poverty, and every kind of financial loss. If He provided release every seven years for indebted slaves in Israel, then you can believe that in living under a better covenant, the blood of Jesus, He will deliver you.

Do you expect God to conform to your logic? To work according to your ability to make money or not? God is a supernatural God. He is not bound by natural circumstances. He works miracles in every realm of life for those who call on Him and believe Him. God supersedes any natural law of finance to work His miracles of prosperity in your life. He can step into your situation in an instant with supernatural provision that supersedes your logic.

Scripture says that when God delivered the Israelites from their bondage in Egypt, they plundered the Egyptians. That nation was so glad to get rid of those slaves that they freely gave them gold, silver, jewelry, livestock, and anything else they asked of them. God's people left their land of slavery rich in goods and money.

Your release can be just as dramatic. Don't think that what you have achieved financially is the best you can do. Dare to believe God's desire to release you to His increase. Begin to declare, "My best work is yet to come. My greatest success is still to be achieved. My best days are ahead of me. God is able to take me into His promised land of blessing and purpose beyond my wildest dreams."

I don't believe everyone is destined to become a millionaire. That is the teaching of some who endorse what I call "hyper-prosperity." But neither does God want you to live in financial lack, having to worry about not having enough for your next mortgage payment or to buy food for your children. If you honor God, He will honor you and provide for your needs.

FOUR LEVELS OF FINANCIAL REALITY

As you learn to be a good manager of God's blessings, He has promised to increase them in your life. He doesn't just want you to gain wealth to use on your own pleasure. You cannot judge your righteousness or spirituality by how much wealth you have. Gain is not godliness. If that were true, the Mafia would be considered godly. God gives prosperity to help you fulfill His purposes in the earth.

Scripture teaches that it is possible to live on four different levels of financial reality. God wants to move you from the lowest level to the highest as you put your faith in His promises for supernatural provision.

1. The bag level

Have you ever had a hole in your pocket and not known it? If you put money in it, you lost it. Haggai told the people that they were working hard but living without enough to eat or drink (Hag. 1). They didn't have enough clothes to wear or to keep them warm. What was the problem? He said it was that they were holding on to what they made, thinking only of themselves and neglecting the house of God. They were violating God's principles of generosity and giving.

Do you have a bag-level mentality? Are you earning and saving and trying to hold on to all your money? Just when you think you are getting ahead, something happens to your car. Or you get sick and have unexpected medical bills. It seems as if there is a hole in your pocket, and you never have enough.

Many live in this bag level of financial reality. It's a place of lack, a place where you never have enough. It says, "I am keeping everything I get; I am bagging it up." People with this mentality think that to get ahead they have to hold on selfishly to every penny. They are bound by greed and dishonesty.

Are you living on the level of financial reality where there is never enough? Holding on to everything you get will keep you in a place of lack because it violates God's principles of giving. You need to learn the secret of getting free from this financial bondage by giving, even in your time of financial lack. The good news is that you don't have to stay on the bag level. You can be released to enjoy God's increase in your personal finances.

2. The barrel level

In Jesus's teachings about money He taught that those who were faithful in a little would be faithful in much (Luke 16:10). That principle is the key to learning to live in the barrel level of blessing. When all you have is a little, you have to learn to give a little. You have to overcome your fear of not having enough. Sowing seed for a harvest is the secret to reaping that harvest.

During the famine in Israel that was announced by Elijah, God told Elijah to leave the brook where He had fed him supernaturally by ravens. He told him to go and find a widow in Zarephath who would provide for him (1 Kings 17).

When Elijah found the widow, he asked her to bring him some water and a morsel of bread. She told him that she did not have any bread. She had a handful of flour in the barrel and a little oil in a jar. She was gathering sticks to cook it for her and her son to eat it and die.

Elijah said to her, "*Do not fear*; go and do as you have said, but make me a small cake from it first, and bring it to me" (v. 13, emphasis added). Then he told her that if she did that, the promise of God to her was that the barrel of flour would not be used up or the jar of oil run dry until the famine was over.

So the widow made a cake for Elijah first. She used everything she had to give to God's servant as he had asked. She and her son survived the famine for many days with the flour and oil that was supernaturally refilled in the barrel and jar.

If you want to get out of the bag level into the barrel level, you are going to have to let fear go and act in faith. You have to give in the face of your own need. It is not logical. Why would you give when you don't have enough for yourself? Because that puts you into miracle territory. Miracles happen in miracle territory! That is the place where you give in faith in obedience to God.

Elijah told the widow to make him a cake first. He was saying to her, "Move into miracle territory!" The moment she obeyed, she moved from bag level of not having enough to barrel level of having just enough. She sowed one cake in obedience, and God gave her a miraculous harvest that met her needs every day until the famine ended.

I like to imagine her friends coming to her home to see this widow open her barrel and take out another day's supply of meal. They watched her go to her empty jar of oil and pour out enough for that day's baking. They saw a

> Why would you give when you don't have enough for yourself? Because that puts you into miracle territory. Miracles happen in miracle territory!

supernatural miracle of God's provision. She told them the story again about making her last cake for the prophet who asked her to give to him first. They gave thanks to God for teaching her how to move into miracle territory through giving.

If you are living in the bag level, God wants you to move into the barrel level, where you have enough to pay bills and provide for your family. That widow was eating her last meal. She did not have enough to survive another day until she gave to the prophet in obedience. Then God prospered her on a new level of miraculous provision. It was just enough, but that was so much better than not having enough.

The barrel level is a blessing of God to keep you from financial lack. You need to be thankful that God has given you enough—that you have enough for your bills, that you have a home and car and the necessities of life. Thank God that you are not living on the bag level. You have moved into miracle territory by learning to give in obedience to God's principles.

However, I don't believe God wants you to stay at the place where you have just enough to pay your bills and meet your family's needs. It is still selfish to think only of yourselves and your needs. You cannot help those less fortunate when you live with just enough for yourselves in your barrel. God wants you to know His great giving heart of generosity—being able to give to the needs of others.

If you have been stuck at the barrel level, where at the end of the month you make all your payments but have nothing left over, you need to ask God to move you to the third level of financial reality: the basket level.

3. The basket level

Do you remember the little boy who offered his lunch to Jesus to feed the multitude? He got up that morning and put five little loaves of bread and two fish in his lunch basket. Then he followed the crowd to hear a Galilean by the name of Jesus preach (John 6:1–12; see also Mark 6:36).

The Bible says that after Jesus had taught the multitude of more than five thousand people, they were hungry. Jesus asked His disciples to feed them. They were astonished at the suggestion to feed all those people. Their answer was to send them away. They told Jesus that all the food they had seen was a little boy's lunch of five loaves of bread and two fish. Jesus told them to bring it to Him.

The Bible says that Jesus took the loaves and fish and did three things: He blessed them, broke them, and gave them to the people. This is the same three-step process that you must go through if you want to fulfill the purposes of God for your life.

First, He takes you out of sin, sets you free, and blesses you. This is the part of the process we love. It feels so good to be free from sin and to have the blessing of God on our lives. Then He begins the breaking process to change our thinking, our selfish desires, and our wrong choices. That is the part we want to skip. But He is breaking you because He wants to "give" you to the people.

God wants to make you a blessing to others, to your community, and even to the nations of the world. When that little boy offered his lunch to the Master, Jesus blessed his basket and used it to satisfy his whole community. All the people were fed from the miraculous multiplication of that little lunch, and there were twelve basketfuls left over!

I think there were twelve basketfuls so that each of the disciples could carry one. I like to imagine that little boy going home to his mother with the disciples following him. His mother sees them and asks what has happened. He says he went to hear Jesus and gave Him his lunch to feed five thousand people. These twelve basketfuls were left over from when Jesus blessed his lunch. They had food for many days to come.

When you give what you have to God, who is the rightful owner, He will bless it and multiply it to meet every need. God wants to move you personally and the entire body of Christ from the barrel level of having just enough to the basket level of providing for the needs of others.

After that community was blessed, the little boy showed up at home with basketfuls left over! If you are living in the barrel level of having just enough, you need to know there is another level that is more than enough! God wants to release you to increase.

One of my family's most memorable Christmases was when we were able to give extravagantly to a deserving family. Our church had several Christmas trees on the stage as decoration during the Christmas season. One of our pastors told me that a single mother of three children had asked if she could just borrow one of those trees for her children's Christmas.

I investigated her situation and realized that she was genuinely trying to give her children all she could on her limited income. She had recently suffered a divorce because of domestic violence and an abusive relationship.

So, on Christmas Eve, my wife and children went with me to Toys "R" Us and began to do Christmas shopping for this family. My children picked out gifts for the children, and we bought decorations and a Christmas tree for them. We arrived at their home with trucks full of gifts for this family. When we delivered all the packages and decorations, we turned to leave. Once outside the apartment, we heard this mother begin to shout her thanksgiving to God. We listened to the squeals of the children, and our hearts were warmed with gratitude to God that we were blessed to bless others.

We need to become people who are looking to bless others. Then God will increase our basket level until it reaches the fourth level of financial reality—the barn level.

4. The barn level

If God can trust you with more than enough so that you are able to give to others, He will move you to an even greater level of prosperity. God wants you to think BIG! You are completely victorious over your fear of financial failure when you understand that your prosperity is for a purpose. Wealth is not about becoming "fat cats." It is about becoming a blessing to others.

When Joseph was delivered from prison and appointed by Pharaoh as the second in command in Egypt, God used him to create food storage centers that would preserve nations during a time of famine. The barns of food that Joseph stored during the seven good years of harvest helped feed the whole world during the seven bad years of famine.

God wants to raise some of you to the barn level. He knows that if He gets it *to* you, He can get it *through* you to touch people all over the world with the truth of the gospel as well as with material blessing.

There are people in my church whom I have pastored for twenty years who were living between the bag and barrel levels years ago. They were hardworking and learning to give out of their need. Now they have become multimillionaires who continue to give more and more to reaching lost souls with the gospel.

God did not move them from bag level to barn level overnight. They went through His process of giving themselves to Him and allowing Him to break them to use them for His purposes. Out of that brokenness He is pouring His blessing through lives. The secret of moving from the bag level of not having enough to the barn level of having enough for the nations, in a word, is obedience.

No matter what level of financial reality you are living in, God already has more than enough for your needs. You don't have to fear your financial situation. God knows how to move you from financial lack to abundance. The only thing that can limit you is your own faith level. When God says move, you have to act in faith to move into His miracle territory.

You may say, "Well, I am retired and live on a fixed income." Not in God. That is not a limitation to God when you move in faith to what He asks you to do. "Well, the economy is down." Do you remember the woman living in famine? Her famine was over when she obeyed what the prophet told her to do, to give first out of her need.

> God knows how to move you from financial lack to abundance. The only thing that can limit you is your own faith level.

You may be about to give birth to a miracle. It is time to get out of the level of lack or of just getting by and allow God to release into your life His resources. If you will obey God and quit holding on to what you have, He will release His provision into your hands so that you can bless others.

I understand that some have taken the principles of prosperity to the extreme. I do not believe in that, but I do believe in prosperity with a purpose. I believe what the Bible teaches about the law of sowing and reaping, and I believe Jesus's teaching about giving.

He did not only teach giving; He gave His life to break the curse of sin over your life. He died to give you an abundant life—not just for eternity, but also for now. He wants to bless you and make you a blessing to others.

The Bible warns against greed and the love of money, calling the love of money the root of all evil (1 Tim. 6:10). You need to guard against loving money more than you love God. God wants to bless your life not just with money, but also with great love for Him and for His Word. He wants to give you His love for the lost souls in the world. When you seek God first and walk in His commandments, He will release supernatural resources into your life.

One of my favorite psalms is Psalm 112, which lists all the blessings God wants to give to us. The prerequisite of receiving His blessings is to walk in the fear of the Lord and delight in His commandments. I fear God. I reverence God and honor Him. I take His Word seriously. According to His Word, God delights in the person who does that.

He delights in you when you read His Word and love it with all your heart. Speak His Word, and walk in His commandments. Begin to say, "I know that God wants to bless me." His promises to you are powerful when you love Him. Your children will be mighty and blessed. You will not be afraid of evil tidings because you are trusting in the Lord. You will guide your affairs with discretion, and you will triumph over your enemies. (See Psalm 112, THE MESSAGE.)

Fear of lack, fear of not having enough is a terrible enemy. God does not want you to live your life on the bag level. His will is to bless you to be a blessing to others.

A testimony of grace

When I first began to pastor Free Chapel, I decided we would not have a bag mentality, meaning we would not ignore the needs of the poor and destitute in our community and in the world. We began to feed the poor and minister to the needy. We determined to become a church characterized by generosity that would give millions of dollars to world missions.

There were times when we were in major building programs and needed money for our concerns. The bag mentality says to satisfy first the needs of your own and to clutch the moneybag to yourself without helping others. But during those times we continued to give, and we increased more and more. As we continued to give, we progressed from a mentality of not having enough to having more than enough. Today our ministry is totally debt free, and we are able to give like never before.

By God's grace we have left the bag level behind and are living in the barn level that is able to supply for the needs of others. God spoke to us to tithe on the income from our television ministry and give to the nations. Our church is taking resources to Haiti to feed impoverished children there. We are working with a malnutrition center to give millions of meals to the neediest children every year. We will be doing the same in Africa as well.

In our area we support Freedom From Addiction ministries for men, women, and teens. Other outreach ministries are being funded out of our barn-level resources as a church. Why does God give us the ability to get wealth? So that He can establish His covenant on the earth. He wants us to take the gospel to every creature.

If you want to have a new beginning in the area of finances and successfully combat your fear of financial lack, please pray this prayer with all your heart:

> *Dear God, thank You for Your wonderful promises to care for Your children as a heavenly Father. I come to embrace Your Word and to seek first Your kingdom. I renounce a spirit of poverty and ask You to release Your levels of prosperity in my life as I obey Your Word. Help me to give with a generous heart. Don't let me stop at having just enough, but allow me the privilege of giving to others as well. I believe You will show me the strategies I need for my employment and my business to combat any financial*

challenge that I will face now or in the future. Keep me from covetousness and greed, and make me a blessing to my community and beyond. Amen.

5

FEARLESS ABOUT YOUR FAMILY

IT IS OBVIOUS that the top priority of Satan's attack in the twenty-first century is your family. If your family is the enemy's top priority, shouldn't it be yours also? In these difficult times you must fight for the values that you cherish and the biblical and moral lifestyles you have dedicated yourself to. A child is the only thing a man and woman can create that is eternal. When you hold that little baby that God gave you in your arms, you are holding an eternal soul. It will be alive one thousand years from now, spending eternity somewhere. You must fight for the soul of that child no matter what attack of the enemy comes against it.

Does fear grip your heart when you see your children struggling with peer pressure? With the temptation to give in to destructive lifestyles? Don't allow fear to overcome you. Instead, you need to fight for your family in prayer. God is with you and will work miracles for you when you pray for your family.

Cherise and I have fought and continue to fight for our family. The world is not going to invade our home without us knowing it. We are constantly making ourselves aware of what our children are doing. Any parent who retreats in times like these, sticking their head in the proverbial sand, will witness hell invading their home. Through watching and prayer, we can keep our children safe.

When television, Internet, and social media platforms such as Facebook, Instagram, and Twitter provide your children with twenty-four-hour instant access to the world, as parents you cannot be neutral or absent in your children's lives. You have to fight the enemy's plans for their destruction. It does no good to worry; you have to war.

As parents of five children, my wife and I are constantly checking computers, tablets, phones, and other gadgets. My kids know that I am paying for their cell phones and that I will read their text messages. They know they cannot have any secret codes that I cannot monitor. As my wife says,

"Our children do not have a private life." We are actively guarding their minds and hearts from evil to maintain our home as a safe place for them to grow up.

Vigilance is key, but you must not live in fear of what your children will experience as they grow. I love what a visiting minister once told our congregation. He said, "I'm convinced that we can't keep our children from their testimonies. When one of my children was trying some crazy stuff, God told me to tell people who asked about that child, 'He's working on his testimony.'"

When God delivers you from evil, He gives you a testimony. When your children are tempted to sin, you can call on God, engage in the fight of faith, and watch their greatest temptation turn into a glorious testimony. If you will fight, God will fight for you.

When you choose to live righteously and embrace the faith fight, God will fight for your family. He will help you to prepare a safe place where you can ride out the flood of iniquity that is rising in the land. You have to fight the good fight of faith and fearlessly face down every threat to your family.

A Tribute to My Parents' "Safe Place"

I am in the ministry today because of the godly home my parents established for my siblings and me. They taught us how to pray and to read and cherish God's Word. They taught us to respect the house of God even as little children.

As a little boy I wanted nothing more than to play with my friends at church. I remember one Sunday when I was about nine years old. My parents pastored a little church in Henderson, North Carolina. When the regular organist was not there, my mother had to play the organ. That left me free to sit in the back of the church with my friends.

One Sunday morning Mom was playing the organ, and my friends and I were sitting in the back. Someone had brought a little mirror, and we noticed that the sun was streaming into the church through the windows. So we decided to have some fun with that mirror.

We would hold it just right to reflect the sunbeam onto the mirror and then into the eyes of the choir members in the front of the church. We could see them singing, and then, all of a sudden, one would go blind because of the laser beam of sunshine we shot at their eyes. We were having the biggest time you could imagine. We were laughing and completely absorbed in our little scheme.

I didn't even notice that my mother had left the organ and was marching to the back of the sanctuary where I was sitting. Suddenly I felt someone grab my shoulder and start leading me out of the pew into the aisle. When I realized it was my mother, I felt like shouting out, "Pray, saints, pray!"

On the way out of the sanctuary Mom pinched my shoulder and said, "I think the devil has got hold of you." I said back to her desperately, "I think he has too," meaning no disrespect. Too late I realized that was not the right thing to say. I will spare you the rest of the story, except to say I knew I was in for good motherly discipline because of my disrespect for the house of God.

My parents maintained a safe place for me, training me and correcting me so that I learned to walk in the fear of God. They simply said no to the culture's advice to "just compromise and let them do what they want to do." Every time they did that, my parents were strengthening my safe place. Every time they imposed their godly standards on my choices and lifestyle, they were rescuing me from the flood of destruction that was all around me.

Even in my teenage years when I tried to rebel, Mom and Dad prayed more for me. They did the same for my two brothers and two sisters. When one of us would begin to stray from the godly principles they taught us, we knew they were fighting for us. We always had family meals together, and if Dad, who loved to eat, was not at the table, we knew he was fasting for one of us. It was a big deal. Mom and Dad usually fasted and prayed together for their children.

Usually when I tried to sin, I could not do it successfully. Others would get by with things, and I would always get caught. One day I went with a friend and tried to get high. I smoked five joints before I could feel just a little of the "joy."

Normally when people get high, they start talking about seeing pink elephants and gorgeous psychedelic colors. Not me. In my pitiful high state I saw Moses, the four horses of the Apocalypse, and other dreadful sights!

When you fight for your kids in prayer, those prayers have an impact! Perhaps like me, your child won't even be able to enjoy partying. It is hard to go out and enjoy sin when you are surrounded by angels assigned to you by your godly parents. They messed me up. Even while I was sleeping, they were praying for me. They fought for my soul, and today I am profoundly grateful.

According to my personality, I could have easily become an alcoholic. When I do something, I go all the way. Social drinking would have led me into alcoholism. When drugs and alcohol were confronting my young life, my parents' values and lifestyle that had formed my character to that point helped me make the right choices.

When promiscuity was presented as a legitimate option to seeking God for a life partner, the moral principles that were part of my foundation stood there protecting me. I thank God today because when the flood of evil came against my immaturity, there was a restraining force inside of me. It told me, "There will be consequences if you choose to do evil." My parents had done their task of creating a godly perspective and a righteous atmosphere that became a powerful standard for my conduct.

When they fought for God's destiny for my life, God fought for them. Today I am grateful to them for their perseverance in prayer. They are the force behind my ministry. They won the fight for my destiny. They were not afraid because they understood that God was fighting for them.

Years later, when I was called to ministry and began fasting and praying a lot, I asked the Lord why He was so hard on me. He answered me and said, "Because your mother is so hard on Me." I understood that if we will be hard on God through prayer and intercession for our children and grandchildren, God will be hard on them. He will intervene in their lives and keep them from evil.

As mothers and fathers, you need to fight for your children in prayer. Don't sit around in fear of what their future holds. Don't be afraid that sin might destroy their lives. Stand up in faith and fight for your family, and God will fight for you.

How to Fight for Your Family

Nehemiah, an Old Testament hero, teaches us how to fight for our families. He was leading Israel in rebuilding the walls of Jerusalem when some enemies showed up and began to threaten their lives. They tried to frighten the people, but Nehemiah challenged the families of Israel:

Don't be afraid of them. Remember the
Lord, who is great and awesome, and *fight
for your brothers, your sons and your
daughters, your wives and your homes.*
—NEHEMIAH 4:14, NIV, EMPHASIS ADDED

Their enemies mocked them and despised their
efforts to make Jerusalem safe again. Then they
determined to attack these Jewish families, forming
a secret plot to destroy them. But rather than being
intimidated, the Jews protected each other as
Nehemiah taught them to defend themselves.

Nehemiah instructed one-half of them to work
to build the wall while the other half stood guard.
Those who were working used one hand to build
and the other to carry a
weapon. They guarded the
city day and night. This
constant vigilance was
necessary to keep them
safe.

I can see myself as a
father standing on that
wall with a trowel for building in one hand and a
weapon in the other. I am determined to build a
successful home and family, even in a time when

> As mothers and fathers,
> you need to fight for
> your children in prayer.
> Don't sit around in
> fear of what their
> future holds. Don't be
> afraid that sin might
> destroy their lives.

half of marriages end in divorce. When statistics say kids have to go through all kinds of dangerous problems, I am going to have kids who serve the Lord. I am fighting for my children, and God is fighting with me.

As you work to build walls of righteousness to protect your home, you have to arm yourselves. You have to decide you are not going to let the enemy have your family. You have to determine, "I'm going to fight for my marriage. I'm going to fight for my children. I'm going to fight the good fight—and win!"

Fighting for our five children

As our children get older, Cherise and I are as determined as ever to fight for them. It seems that evil is more intense, the culture is more corrupt, and the influences of worldliness that bombard our children are even more powerful than when I was a child.

One summer we planned a family trip to the beach. Our teenage girls invited some of their girlfriends to go with them. Some other families from our church happened to be at the beach that same week. Their teenage boys were friends with our girls. So, when we arrived at the beach, we sat our girls down and laid the ground rules for what was acceptable behavior at the beach with their friends.

One thing that was not to be tolerated was for our girls to go down to the beach at night with a member of the opposite sex. We wanted to be clear to everyone concerned, so we said, "Got it?" "Yes, Dad. Got it."

Then one evening, while my wife and I were absorbed in a movie, our telephone rang. One of our daughters was there with us, and she answered the phone. I paid no attention, but her mother pricked up her ears. When my wife realized that she was talking with her older sister on the phone, she became very interested. She heard our younger daughter say, "Yes, they are sitting right here."

That was suspicious! Her mother asked her who she was talking to, and she responded meekly that it was her older sister. Her mother whispered threateningly, "You tell me everything she said, or I will take your phone away for a year!" She glanced up at her mother's face and promised quickly, nodding.

After further consultation with our daughter about the phone call, my wife came to drag me away from my movie. She said we were going to take a walk down to the beach. I moaned and resisted, but she insisted. There was no saying no to that tone in her voice.

Then, instead of taking the normal walk to the beach, she led me through bushes and made me crawl on all fours, jump over a fence, and sneak all the way to the beach in the dark! Sure enough, we found our teenage girls there with boys from other families of the church.

One of the boys saw us coming and almost went into shock. He started fidgeting, and his face turned white. He couldn't think of anything to say, so he said, "Hello, Pastor. That was a great sermon last Sunday." I was not smiling. I just said, "Aw, shut up! You don't even know what I preached. Get your tail off this beach now!"

He knew he was busted, though apparently the kids had done nothing wrong, except break the rules. He put his head down and said, "Sorry, Pastor," as he walked off. My daughters knew the rules, and after speaking to them briefly, we took them back to the cabin where we emphatically made them aware of their "safe place," to the end that they would never forget!

Training, teaching, staying in their lives, and

refusing to compromise—it is all part of fighting for your family and seeing God fight for you. Building a safe place against the evil influences of society that try to tempt, coerce, and deceive your children is a full-time job.

STRATEGY FOR A HEALTHY HOME

No one said that building a healthy, godly family would be easy. You must be committed to winning the war that rages against your home. The battle is relentless for parents who want to establish godly foundations for your family. You can't let up your vigil. It takes time and energy to stay in your children's lives.

Do you feel overwhelmed by their peer influences? Does the fear of drugs, alcohol, and illicit sex grip your heart for your children? Fighting against destructive forces that threaten your family means you have to call on God to fight for you. Don't be intimidated by the enemy's threats; don't just sit back and let it happen. Make up your mind to work together as parents, and support each other in the fight.

My wife and I learned that we had to settle two things as a young couple. First, that we loved God.

And second, that we were totally committed to each other. That means that we are committed to the church, that we fill our lives with the Word of God continually, and that we determine to raise a godly family together.

That is what all married couples need to do. There might be times when you disagree and get your feelings hurt. You might say harsh things to each other, but you have to be determined to forgive and work it out. Obey the Word of God, show mercy, and strive to live in peace.

You need to tell the enemy that he has no right to your home, your children, or your marriage. I am not afraid to raise our five children in these uncertain times, because I know that as we submit our lives to God and fight for our family, God is fighting for us.

You have to build your home with a weapon in one hand and a trowel in the other constantly. Grab your divine weapons—the name of Jesus, the Word, prayer, and praise—in one hand. Take a building instrument in the other hand, and be prepared to fight and build as the occasion arises. Begin to declare in the taunting face of the enemy, "I'm going to rebuild, and I'm going to fight until I get the victory in my own home." Speak the name of Jesus, declare the promises of God's Word, and praise Him for the victory that is coming.

If you are a single parent, you are entitled to the same protection of the promises of God for your family. It is your responsibility to fight for your family, whatever your circumstances. You need to know that you are not alone. If you submit your life to God in prayer and fasting, you will see Him preserve your children from the destructions of the enemy.

When the enemy tries to attack my family, I declare to him what Nehemiah declared to his enemies:

> The God of heaven, he will prosper us...but ye have no portion, nor right, nor memorial, in Jerusalem.
>
> —NEHEMIAH 2:20, KJV

We don't have to be afraid of what hell can do to our children. I am aware that even if I bring them up right in the fear of the Lord, hell may have a shot at them. But when it's all said and done, they know where the altar is; they know to call on the name of Jesus. And I know that He is the preserver of my home and my children; He will fight for my family.

The Word of God promises protection against the purposes of the enemy for those who choose to obey His will. The prophet Isaiah declared, "No weapon that is formed against thee shall prosper.... This is the heritage of the servants of the LORD, and their righteousness is of me, saith the LORD" (Isa. 54:17, KJV).

PERSEVERING IN THE FIGHT

Nehemiah taught the people how to fight continually for their sons and their daughters. God will prosper you and fight for you when you declare that the enemy does not have any right to your "Jerusalem"—your home and family. He cannot touch your wife. Your children do not belong to him. He has no portion in your home.

Not only did Israel win the fight for their families, but they also preserved the safety of future generations. Did you know that portions of the wall Nehemiah and Israel restored are still standing in Jerusalem today? I have been to Israel five times and have seen parts of the Jerusalem wall that date back to the rebuilding that Nehemiah directed. Their perseverance in the battle for their families gave them victory that is still evident thousands of years later.

When you build a safe place for your children, you are building multigenerational foundations upon which your grandchildren and future generations can stand. The psalmist asked the question, "If the foundations are destroyed, what can the righteous do?" (Ps. 11:3). But if you will fight, God will fight for you to keep the foundations of righteousness for your children's children and beyond.

For that to be a reality, however, you must set a guard in your home to protect it from any sneaky plan of the enemy. You cannot allow the immorality projected through any kind of media into your home. That gives the enemy access to your home. You have to protect your family from profane and unclean speech, music, or other destructive forces that try to invade your home. As I've said, this requires a continual vigil and perseverance in your fight for your family's well-being.

You may not always be the most popular person in your home. Your goal is not to be popular; you are not supposed to be a buddy or best friend to your children. You are their protector from evil when they cannot discern its presence because of their immaturity.

When Noah heard the word of God to build an ark to preserve his family from destruction, he obeyed God completely. He spent over a century working to build an ark of safety for his family. Not only did he get the animals on board, but he made sure his entire family was safely on board that ark as well. The New Testament refers to Noah as the eighth person on the ark (2 Pet. 2:5, KJV). I believe that refers to the fact that Noah was the last person to board the ark.

He did not just throw down the gangplank and board that ark, hoping the other seven members of his family would go with him. Noah was the eighth person, the last one aboard. He was not just going to be rescued himself. He determined that his kids were going with him. They were the reason for his one hundred twenty years of labor on the ark. They were part of the covenant God made with him, and he

> You are not supposed to be a buddy or best friend to your children. You are their protector from evil when they cannot discern its presence because of their immaturity.

was responsible for their well-being. He made sure they went with him into the safety of that ark.

I am disturbed at the way people just give up and relinquish their children to the enemy. They take a "what's the use?" attitude when their children are tempted to sin. Or they adopt an "I hope they make it" perspective. That is a cowardly way to face the onslaught of the enemy against your family. They are worth fighting for. They are eternal souls entrusted into your care.

The Bible says that Job offered ten sacrifices every day, one for each of his ten children (Job 1). I believe he called the name of each child as he made a sacrifice for them. Through the blood of the sacrificed animal, he was putting a hedge of protection around them, fighting for his family every day.

Every day I pray for my children by name. I ask God to put a hedge around them with His Son's blood. I pray for their protection and their cleansing from any evil thing they might encounter. You need to plead the blood of Jesus over your children daily. The blood of Jesus does two things: it cleanses and it protects your home. You can build a protective hedge around your children by applying the blood of Jesus over them in prayer.

Even if your children are away from the Lord right now, you mustn't give up praying for their salvation and protection. In fact, now more than ever you need to fight for them. Continue praying until the day you see them return to the Lord.

God has given you the privilege and the responsibility to raise your children. You must fight for your sons and your daughters. Fight for your husband. Fight for your wife. Fight for your daughters-in-law and your sons-in-law. Put on the whole armor of God (Eph. 6), and declare to the enemy, "You just stepped onto holy ground when you attacked my home. I'll fight you to hell and back for my babies."

How will you live your life? Will you fill it with work and activities so that someone else has to care for your family? MTV is not going to raise my babies. Babysitters are not going to raise my babies. Schools are not going to raise my babies. My wife and I are going to raise our babies in the fear of the Lord.

Give yourself and your home to God, and He will give you wisdom and power to protect your children.

You don't have to live in fear for your children. God will redeem them for His purposes. You are not alone. God is with you. Even if you are a single parent, you can rest assured that God's protection is enough for your children and you.

I believe that the devil's number one priority is to destroy your home. He wants to make it miserable; he wants to tear it to pieces. The Lord wants you to understand that if your home is the enemy's first priority, it must be your first priority. Not your ministry. Not your career. Not recreation or the accumulation of "things." Nothing should be more important in your life than maintaining a godly home. Your number one priority is to fight for your family against the attacks of the enemy.

CLEANSING YOUR HOME

To me, one of the most amazing scriptures in the Bible about the home is found in Leviticus 14. When the children of Israel possessed their Promised Land, God told them they would live in homes they did not build. What they did not know is that those homes had been dedicated to idols.

These pagan people lived idolatrous, ungodly lives and practiced all kinds of unclean acts. They had idols hidden in the walls of their homes. They were unseen by the people but known to God. This pagan idolatry caused streaks to appear on the walls that could only be cleansed by a blood sacrifice.

God told Moses that when they saw greenish or reddish streaks on the walls, the house was contaminated and had to be cleansed by blood. They had to call a priest to come and make sacrifice for their home.

These streaks on the walls were called fretting leprosy. The word *fretting* relates to anger and conflict. Is there continual strife and contention in your home? Those are streaks on the wall that have to be cleansed by the blood of Christ. Otherwise your relationships will suffer, and your home will be destroyed.

Verbal and physical abuse are streaks on the wall that must be cleansed by the blood. These hidden things in our homes attract Satan's influence against our families. You can apply the blood of Jesus to your home, and He will give grace for forgiveness and love to rule there. God wants you to experience His peace and joy in your home.

There are other ways believers allow their homes to become contaminated, causing "streaks" on the walls. Many Christian parents allow vile music with violent lyrics into their homes (knowingly or unknowingly through iPods and other devices). Some engage in addictive pornography accessed on the Internet and other kinds of media.

Some homes have allowed books on the occult, violent TV programs, and ungodly movies to have access to their homes. They cause streaks on the walls that compromise your godliness. You have to set a standard for what is acceptable to enter your home. Draw lines against your children's exposure to profanity and uncleanness.

Monitor your children's TV programs. Be vigilant about their computer use. As the priest of your home, you must continually cleanse it with the blood of Christ. If you are a single parent, you are the spiritual head of your home. Just as Job offered sacrifices for his children continually, you are responsible to cleanse your home and dedicate it to the Lord continually.

As a parent, I understand how fear can grip your heart for your children's well-being, especially during their teenage years. They are making decisions that can affect their future and their reputations for life. To combat those fears, I have determined to fight for my family. I refuse to worry about them. Through prayer I will make it hard on God, and He will make it hard on them. I make every effort to stay in their lives, listening to their conversations and giving them direction.

ARROWS IN THE HANDS
OF A WARRIOR

The psalmist declared that children are a heritage from the Lord and are like arrows in the hand of a warrior. He said that a man who has his quiver full of them is happy (Ps. 127:3–5). I began to think about arrows and what they need to be effective. This analogy makes me the bow that gives the arrow—the child—direction.

If I point my bow in the direction of alcohol, the arrow will go toward alcohol. If I point it toward getting money as its goal, it will fly toward getting rich. The arrow will go in the direction that I point it. I can't expect the arrow to go toward the church if I am not pointing it in that direction. That is simple logic.

When you teach your children to love God, Scripture says they will not be ashamed. They won't be ashamed of where they go to church or of living moral lives. When you point them toward righteous living, they will become a weapon against the devil's plans for their destruction.

Teach your children that they are not like the family down the street or the friend in school. When they say, "They all do it," tell them you are not like other families. Point their arrow toward holiness, worship, and God's calling for their life to become a pastor, evangelist, teacher, or godly employee or employer. They are destined to become godly parents who will follow your lead.

Sometimes I think we are trading the call and purpose of God in our children's lives for the American dream. We point their arrow toward becoming a professional athlete or a powerful businessman, or toward fame in movies or the arts. We focus on getting them into the right schools and getting them on the right career path so they will earn the best salary possible and be at the top of their field. If God calls them to a career like that to bring honor to Jesus Christ, then that is the right direction for their arrow. But the greatest direction for anyone's arrow is to bring glory and honor to Christ in whatever they do.

You have to "shoot your arrows" toward truth.

Teach them that there is one God. Buddha is not God. Muhammad is not God. New Age philosophies do not replace God. You were created by God to walk in His truth. The apostle John said that nothing could make him happier than getting reports that his children continue diligently in the way of truth (3 John 3, THE MESSAGE).

> Sometimes I think we are trading the call and purpose of God in our children's lives for the American dream.

When you direct your children toward truth, they will understand that money is not God. Education is not God. Sports are not God. Fame is not God. Everything they value will be of God. They will know the name of God's Son, Jesus Christ, and will serve Him. They can't waiver or think there might be another way. The Bible says there is no other name given unto men whereby we can be saved (Acts 4:12).

Continually point them in the direction of truth, and they will defeat every destructive force that comes against them. You have to take charge of those precious arrows in your quiver. It is a continual fight to keep them going in the right direction, but you can be fearless as you trust God to take care of them. God will fight for you when you decide to fight for your family. Pray with me that God will help you begin or intensify your battle to maintain a safe place for your family:

Dear Jesus, thank You for my family. Thank You for opening my eyes to see that You want my home to be a safe place—an ark—to give refuge against the floodwaters of sin that threaten our world today. Help me to make my family the priority that You intend it to be. I repent for being afraid to face the problems I see in my home. I determine to fight for my family, knowing that You will fight for me. Holy Spirit, please show me every unclean thing that needs to be cleansed from my life and home. I refuse to worry or be afraid. Through intercession I will make it hard on You, God, and You will make it hard on them. Thank You. Amen.

6

FEARLESS ABOUT YOUR HEALTH

LIFE EXPECTANCY IN the United States has nearly doubled during the twentieth century. We are better able to cure and control diseases than any other civilization in history.[1] Yet the media paint a different picture of our nation's health. In 1996 Bob Garfield, a magazine writer, reviewed articles about serious diseases published over the course of a year in the *Washington Post*, the *New York Times*, and *USA Today*. From his reading he learned:

- Fifty-nine million Americans had heart disease.

- Fifty-three million suffered with migraines.

- Twenty-five million had osteoporosis.

- Sixteen million were obese.

- Three million had cancer.

- Ten million suffered from more obscure ailments such as temporo-mandibular joint disorders.

- Two million suffered brain injuries.[2]

Adding up the estimates, Garfield determined that most Americans are seriously sick. "Either as a society we are doomed, or someone is seriously double-dipping," he suggested.[3]

Don't listen to ABC, NBC, and "Woe Is Me" networks. They only try to create a culture of fear, making much ado about nothing. God does not want you to live in chronic fear because of what the media promote, often to sell their products.

I challenge you to use the Word of God as a powerful antidote for anxiety, fear, and panic attacks. Put on the armor of God that the apostle Paul describes, which includes the shield of faith to deflect the darts of the enemy. It also includes the sword of the Spirit, which is the Word of God (Eph. 6:17). Those divine weapons give you supernatural power to live the fearless life. They will release the power of God into every negative situation you face.

OUR PERSONAL HEALTH CRISIS

Our family faced a very scary crisis with our oldest daughter when she went to my wife and told her that she had found a lump in her breast. My wife tells it as only a mother can:

> My grandmother died of breast cancer, and my mother was diagnosed with breast cancer many years ago. I will never forget the day my daughter, then seventeen, came to me and said that she found a lump in her breast. My heart filled with fear immediately, considering our family history. Trying not to scare her, I remained outwardly calm and told her it was probably nothing; girls have knots all the time. But inside I was panicking.
>
> The next day I took her to the doctor to check it out. The doctor found the lump and said it was the size of a quarter. Because of the breast cancer history, he sent us to Atlanta to a specialist and told us it didn't look good. We could not get in

to see the specialist for a week, which was pure torture.

That Wednesday night we had a very powerful service. Our daughter, who was usually at the youth services on Wednesday nights, was in the sanctuary that night singing with the praise team. The Spirit of God fell, and my husband felt prompted to call people forward for prayer.

She walked to the front weeping, along with many others who needed a touch from God that night. Later she said, "When I received prayer, something changed, and I felt the peace of God just engulf me. That terrible life-gripping fear left me."

When we got home, she came to us and said she couldn't find the lump. So we went back to our local doctor that next morning to see if he could find it. He couldn't.

As she lay on the examining table, I said, with concern, "It has to be there. Check again. Keep checking." But he said, "Whatever was there is not there now." So we returned to the specialist to have comprehensive tests done, and there was no lump to be found anywhere. The specialist said simply, "There is nothing there. We don't need to see you again until you are twenty."

In our crisis we cried out to God for our daughter's health. We declared with cold-feet courage that God is her healer. We could have submitted to our fear and subjected her to surgery and other treatment. But God was there for us as we dared to call on Him in our scary crisis.

I wish every story ended with a miracle or healing, but it doesn't always happen that way. Sometimes God takes you through the fiery-furnace experience instead of delivering you from the fiery furnace.

In scary conditions you can calm your fears and fill your heart with courage to face life's challenges by focusing on God's Word. You have to decide to become a warrior and not a worrier. You can use the promises of the Word of God to overcome worry and live fearlessly.

We live in challenging times that will make you into a warrior or a worrier. There will be no middle ground. When you hear bad economic news, are faced with a health crisis, or are tempted to worry about your children, choose to war against fear with God's Word instead of worrying and fearing the worst. When trouble comes, when tough times hit your life, refuse to cower in fear.

What will you do if you receive a bad report from your doctor, if you see the disease on your X-ray, or if you receive a pink slip from your employer? How will you react if you face foreclosure? Whether it is your marriage, your children, your finances, or your health that is in crisis, you have to decide whether to become a worrier or a warrior.

> You have to decide to become a warrior and not a worrier.

I don't understand why people have to go through stuff. I don't understand why cancer attacks good people who have never smoked a day in their lives, or why they must face the side effects of radiation and treatment. What do you do during these hard times? Either you give in to fear and allow it to destroy your peace and well-being, or you become a warrior against it.

Being a warrior doesn't mean you don't ever feel afraid of the uncertainty of everything that could and might happen. But when fear threatens to engulf your mind, begin to declare as David did, "Whenever I am afraid, I will trust in You" (Ps. 56:3).

In that place of declaring your faith, God will be very near to you.

COURAGE WITH COLD FEET

Remember the story of Benaiah I shared earlier? He was a hero during the reign of King David and became one of the king's mighty men. The Bible says that he killed a lion in a pit on a snowy day. He had the courage to jump down into a snowy pit with a lion and fight with him to the death. I call that courage with cold feet!

When we say we have cold feet, we mean we were afraid to do something. Courage is doing what you are afraid to do. It is not taking action without feeling any fear. Someone has said, "Courage is fear that has said its prayers."[4]

When you hear from God and He tells you to do something, you are filled with faith in that moment. It braces your spine like steel. You have heard from God! Then, when you move out in faith, you encounter the lion that is about to attack.

The apostle Peter tells us that we are in warfare with a lion: "Be sober, be vigilant; because your adversary the devil walks about like a roaring lion, seeking whom he may devour" (1 Pet. 5:8). That is

147

when you get courage with cold feet. But it's all right. Mark Twain said, "Courage is resistance to fear, mastery of fear—not absence of fear."[5]

God needs some men and women in these troubled times to have the courage to say, "God said to do it, and I am going to do it!" Even if you have to get into knee-deep snow and fight a lion, you say, "Bring it on! I will not retreat in fear, because I know what God told me! I may have courage with cold feet, but the lion is not going to conquer me; I am going to conquer him!" The fact is, there is no real courage unless you are scared!

UNEQUAL FIGHTS

If you are going to fight a lion, it would seem better to pick a warm sunshiny day rather than a cold snowy one. But we don't choose the timing of the fight—the enemy does—and it is an unequal fight. There is nothing equal about a lion and a man fighting. Obviously the lion is stronger and has the advantage, but God is known for putting His people into unequal fights.

There was nothing equal about Jehoshaphat and his army marching into the flashing steel of the Syrian army with their praise team on the front line. He obviously never studied war strategy at West Point. It would give a five-star general a coronary arrest to think that he had to put musical instruments in his frontline army marching into enemy territory. What military officer would consider trying to defeat the enemy with a violin, harp, and tambourine?

There is nothing equal about the children of Israel marching around the impregnable walls of Jericho as a war strategy—or with David and his slingshot against the giant Goliath. But your "nothingness" plus God's "almightiness" equals giants falling down, walls falling down, armies ambushing themselves, and victory in every battle He gives you to fight. So be of good courage.

You might feel that you are no match for the diagnosis you've been given. You may feel that this situation is going to do you in. But I have good news for you: when you are facing insurmountable odds, that's the realm of fearlessness. That is the place for courage with cold feet.

I have been there, friend! When God told me to go to Gainesville to pastor Free Chapel, I went in courage with cold feet. When He said to build a church building, two and a half million dollars seemed like twenty-nine million dollars. Our congregation moved forward in courage with cold feet. Then when we bought more land for five million dollars, we had to summon courage to conquer our fear again. And when we began to build a sanctuary for seventeen million dollars, I said, "Here I am again, moving forward in courage with cold feet."

If your courage has cold feet right now, begin to remind yourself of the times in your life when God has come through for you in what seemed like impossible situations. Think about other times when you've stepped out in faith and He has been right there to meet your need. Encourage yourself in the Lord. Get all the second, third, and fourth opinions about your condition that you need. Make sure you know all your options. But then pray and ask God for wisdom in how to approach your treatment. Then when you've "done all," the Bible says, "Stand." Stand with courage, knowing you can trust Him completely.

When you do this, let me tell you what happens. When you get out there into the realm of the miraculous and have done all to stand in what God said, you begin to see miracles. Miracles happen in miracle territory.

God responds to courage that is demonstrated in the midst of fear. You can win your "unequal" battle with fearlessness.

You have to decide to take the Word of God and His promises, believing His great love for you, and go to war with those weapons. He will give you the courage if you choose to overcome your fear and fight for your victory, for your family's victory, and for whatever "unequal" fight the enemy has designed against you. Don't give in to worrying. Declare that you are a warrior, and say in the face of your lion, "It is written..." I encourage you to pray this prayer as you determine to be a victorious warrior:

> *Dear Jesus, forgive me for allowing my mind to be filled with fear. Help me to become a warrior instead of a worrier. I choose to obey Your commands and to go forward in courage even when I feel afraid. I say with David, "What time I am afraid, I will trust." I believe that I will begin to see miracles in my life as I take Your Word and believe Your promises, declaring in the face of the enemy, "It is written." Thank You, Lord. Amen.*

7

FEARLESS ABOUT DEATH
and ETERNITY

EATH STALKS US all. It is a formidable foe. We can try to ignore it, but sooner or later the ball and chain of death yanks all of us back into reality. At first, when we are born, we are fragile. Then for a moment we are strong. Sometimes we are tricked by the resilience of our youth into ignoring our mortality until finally, without fail, we all find the canker of disease gnawing somewhere inside our body. In the end we are frail again—and we die.

Given free rein, the black giant of death would have long since sent this planet hurling through space like an abandoned ship. But in a stable yard at Bethlehem, within earshot of the lowing oxen and under the brilliance of a flaming star, through a teenage peasant girl the antagonist for death was born! Death had reigned supreme for six thousand years, but Jesus conquered it in three days! Rattling the keys of death and hell, Jesus rose on the third day saying, "I am He who lives, and was dead, and behold, I am alive forevermore" (Rev. 1:18).

A legend is told of a missionary in Brazil who discovered a tribe of natives living in a remote part of the jungle next to a large river. The natives were convinced that the river was filled with evil spirits, and consequently they were afraid to cross it. Disease was rampant among their population, and they were dying daily. They desperately needed medicine, or the whole tribe would be wiped out. The only way to get help was to traverse that river they were terrified to cross.

The missionary explained to the tribe that the river was not haunted and was not evil. But it was to no avail. So he reached down into the river, splashing himself with the water and saying to them again: "See, it's not evil. You don't have to be afraid to cross the river." But again, it was to no avail. So he waded out into the river and splashed around.

Looking back at them, he signaled to them to come into the water. But his words fell on deaf ears.

The missionary was so consumed with compassion to see them made well and healed that in desperation he plunged into the black, angry river. He swam beneath the surface until he reached the other side, and when he struggled up onto the shore, he thrust a triumphant fist into the air, facing the natives standing on the other side of the river. When he did that, there was a great shout that rose up, and one after another the tribesmen clambered into the water and began swimming across the river they had feared so much.

The missionary had to become an example of overcoming the terror of that river in order to set free the tribe who feared it. In that same way Jesus Christ, through His death and resurrection, swam the river of our final foe called death. And He has come out triumphantly on the other side! We have nothing to fear! Christ has already made a pathway for us to safely cross over to the other side.

> Forasmuch then as the children are partakers of flesh and blood, he also himself likewise took part of the same; that through death he might destroy him

that had the power of death, that is, the devil; and deliver them who through fear of death were all their lifetime subject to bondage.

—HEBREWS 2:14–15, KJV

Heaven is a place where every house is a mansion, every step is a march in unity, every meal is a banquet, every moment is ecstasy, every hour is rapture, and every day is jubilee. There will be no fevers, no exhausting pain, no hospitals filled with those waiting to die. There will be no sad good-byes.

Here on earth some of us brush back tears, others weep with broken hearts, and still others bid loved ones farewell with quiet resolve. But the Bible says that in heaven, "God will wipe away every tear from their eyes" (Rev. 7:17). It teaches that our last breath here will be our first breath there! And heaven is a place where we'll never say good-bye.

In fact, the Bible says that we cannot imagine how wonderful our life will be in heaven. Jesus told His disciples He was going to prepare a place for them so that they could be where He is (John 14:2). And the apostle Paul said, "Eye has not seen, nor ear heard, nor have entered into the heart of man the things which God has prepared for those who love Him" (1 Cor. 2:9).

The only question that remains for you, personally, to answer is this: Where will I go when I die? The Bible says there are two options for your future in eternity—a state of bliss in heaven, or eternal torment in hell.

Of course, you can choose not to believe the Bible. But if it's true and these are your only two options for living forever after death, that would mean you have a 50 percent chance of being right. What happens if you are wrong? If there is life after death, if heaven and hell are real, what will it be like for you? Should you be filled with dread or anticipation?

SHOULD YOU FEAR DEATH?

According to studies, most people admit to having some anxiety about death. Patterns of death anxiety show that:[1]

- Women tend to report somewhat higher levels of death-related anxiety.

- Older people in general seem to have less death anxiety.

- People with mental and emotional disorders tend to suffer from a higher level of death anxiety.

- Death anxiety can spike temporarily to a higher level for people who have been exposed to traumatic situations.

If you are like most people who do not want to think about death, what causes your greatest anxiety? Fear of a plane crash? A terrorist attack? Of falling from heights? If so, you are not alone. These are some of the most-feared causes of death. However, the likelihood of dying from these causes is remote. Here are the facts:[2]

LIKELIHOOD OF MOST-FEARED CAUSES OF DEATH

The actual risk of death in a plane crash would be once in 19,000 years if you flew on an airplane once a day for 19,000 years.
Between the years 1580 and 2003 there have been 1,909 confirmed shark attacks. The real odds of being killed by a shark are zero in 264.1 million.
Falling deaths are estimated to kill 80 people each year, mainly among those who work at heights in construction.

Historically speaking, you have a one in 9.3 million chance of dying from a terrorist attack.

Death from natural disaster is less likely than being killed by a fire or committing suicide.

One thing is certain: everyone will die. Until Jesus returns as He has promised to do and takes believers to be with Him (1 Thess. 4:17), the only way to leave this world is by dying. The Bible teaches clearly that when that happens, you will face one of two fates: to live eternally in the presence of God, or to live eternally in hell with Satan.

Jesus taught plainly about heaven and hell and made it clear that one of those places would be your eternal destination. He warned:

> And I say to you, My friends, do not be afraid of those who kill the body, and after that have no more that they can do. But I will show you whom you should fear: Fear Him who, after He has killed, has power to cast into hell; yes, I say to you, fear Him!
> —Luke 12:4–5

This is the only time that Jesus told us to fear. After all the "fear nots" He gave to us, He made sure that we knew there was someone we must fear. It was His warning to us in order to avoid eternal damnation. Eternal means "forever, never-ending." The fact is that you will be alive thousands of years from now—somewhere. Should you fear the place where you will be?

HELL IS A PLACE

Hell is one of the most difficult subjects I have to deal with as a minister. I don't enjoy talking about hell. But when I read the words of Jesus, I am constantly reminded that there is a place called hell, and that it is a place of eternal torment. Jesus said the pathway to destruction was very broad and that many would go down that path (Matt. 7:13).

Most people refuse to think about death or eternity. They choose to simply live in denial. They don't think about what it would be like to spend forever in hell, where Jesus said the fire is never quenched (Mark 9:43). That is why Jesus talked so much about hell. He knew people would try to block it out of their minds. The devil would help them do just that by deceiving them, working hard to keep them from believing in Jesus or in hell.

Jesus taught that the justice of God demands a

place be prepared for those who reject His sacrificial death on Calvary. He also said that hell was not prepared for people; it was prepared for the devil and his angels (Matt. 25:41). God does not want anyone to perish (2 Pet. 3:9). That is why Jesus came to die for our sin. Everyone who accepts His forgiveness for sin will escape hell and live in heaven with Him forever.

But it is the devil's goal to take as many people with him as possible into the lake of fire. He works to deceive them into rejecting the salvation that Jesus came to give to all who accept Him as Savior. He tries to get them not to believe in his existence and to mock those who do believe.

> Jesus taught that the justice of God demands a place be prepared for those who reject His sacrificial death on Calvary.

What is the atmosphere of hell?

What is the atmosphere in hell going to be like? That will be determined by the kind of people who go there. The Bible says that drunkards, adulterers, revelers, murderers, idolaters, sorcerers, liars, and every wicked person will be there (Gal. 5:19–21; Rev. 21:8). It is not a happy place. Even if hell wasn't a place of everlasting fire and torment, the inhabitants there would make the atmosphere intolerable.

Jesus described hell in a story of a rich man who enjoyed the good life and lived extravagantly and selfishly. There was a beggar named Lazarus who was laid at his gate, desiring only the crumbs that fell from the rich man's table. He was filled with sores and lived in misery. When the beggar died, the angels carried him to paradise to be with Abraham. After that, the rich man died. Jesus said he was in torment in the flames of Hades.

Then the rich man looked and saw Abraham a long way away, and he asked Abraham to let Lazarus just dip his finger in water and come to cool his tongue. Abraham said that he could not come to him because of the great gulf between them. The rich man wanted someone to go back and warn his five brothers so that they would not come to that place of torment (Luke 16:20–28). That was not possible either. Jesus made it clear from this story that hell is a very real place, and there is no escape from its torment.

Jesus lamented, "For what will it profit a man if he gains the whole world, and loses his own soul?" (Mark 8:36). It wasn't that riches in themselves were evil. But Jesus was saying that if you live for everything the world calls "gain," you could still lose your soul. You must choose to follow Christ on earth in order to spend eternity with Him.

It is possible that PhDs, scientists, doctors, sports icons, music idols, and any other persons of notoriety could lose their souls. No one is exempt from eternal damnation unless they accept salvation provided through the blood of Christ. The Bible says that there is no salvation in any other name (Acts 4:12). Only submission to the lordship of Christ will allow you to escape the horrors of hell and assure you of eternal life in heaven with Him.

Jesus described hell with words like *destruction, damnation, outer darkness, torment,* and *everlasting fire.* Can you imagine living in darkness forever? Wishing for the day? Begging for relief from the flame? You cannot live wrong and die right!

If you are living wrong, you will die wrong and go to a place called hell. It is a place that is void of the presence of God. No light! No love! No peace! No joy! The Bible says that in hell there will be torment day and night, forever and ever (Rev. 20:10).

There are no exits from hell, no time off for good behavior. Once you are there, you have no way out.

That is the choice you make when you are living your life on earth. The dreadful outcome of rejecting Christ is spending eternity in a terrible place, a place called hell. Hell is no joke! Your friends can mock and laugh you into hell, but they can't laugh you out of hell.

The good news is that the Bible says if you repent and accept Christ as your Savior, God blots out all of your sin and does not even remember it (Isa. 43:25). In other words, God says that if you repent, He will think your sins out of existence. He accepts you as His forgiven son or daughter and gives you the privilege of living with Him forever. You exchange the terrible place called hell for the indescribably wonderful place called heaven.

HEAVEN IS A PLACE

Jesus taught that heaven is also a place. Jesus told His disciples He was going to prepare a place for them. He said that in His Father's house there are many mansions. And Jesus promised to take them there to be with Him forever (John 14:1–2).

What is heaven like? The atmosphere of heaven will be the essence of pure love, because God is love (1 John 4:16). It will be filled with light, because there is no darkness in Him. Peace, joy, and righteousness will reign in the light of His love.

The Bible gives us glimpses inside of heaven. On several occasions the heavens open to allow people on earth to see inside. When Jesus was baptized, the heavens were opened to Him, and He saw the Spirit of God descending like a dove and resting on Him (Matt. 3:16). When Stephen was stoned to death, he saw the heavens opened and Christ standing at the right hand of God (Acts 7:56).

Peter also saw heaven open when the Lord gave him a vision to teach him that salvation was for everyone (Acts 10:10–15). The apostle Paul was taken into the third heaven and shown divine secrets that he could not even share (2 Cor. 12:2–4). And the apostle John saw a door standing open in heaven when Jesus showed him things to come in the Book of Revelation (Rev. 4:1).

John saw the New Jerusalem, which is called the City of God. It could be called the capital city of heaven. John was permitted to measure it and found it is square and is fifteen hundred miles on each side and fifteen hundred miles tall. Its foundations are made of precious, transparent stones like sapphire, jasper, and sardonyx. The radiant sun of God's glory shines throughout that beautiful city, dazzling light reflecting through those stones.

The streets of heaven are paved with transparent gold. There is a pure river of water of life, clear as crystal, proceeding from the throne of God. Along the river is the tree of life filled with fruits. And the leaves of the tree were for the healing of the nations (Rev. 22:1–2). We know that there is a magnificent banquet hall in heaven where Jesus will eat the marriage supper of the Lamb with all of His bride, the sons and daughters of God.

These are just glimpses of the wonderful place called heaven, which is promised to all who serve Christ on the earth. It is a place of worship where the Lord of love dwells. And there will be no sorrow or tears there, for He will wipe away all tears. Eternal bliss, living forever with the giver of life, is the reward that awaits you in heaven.

Heaven's reward

We live such few years on earth even if we live to be seventy or eighty or older. Compared to eternity that never ends, there is nothing we have to sacrifice here that is worth missing heaven. The apostle Paul said, "For to me, to live is Christ, and to die is gain" (Phil. 1:21). He seemed almost anxious to leave this world behind to live eternally with his Lord.

When the apostle Paul knew it was time for him to die he said:

> I have fought the good fight, I have finished the race, I have kept the faith. Finally, there is laid up for me the crown of righteousness, which the Lord, the righteous Judge, will give to me on that Day, and not to me only but also to all who have loved His appearing.
>
> —2 TIMOTHY 4:7–8

It was obvious that Paul did not fear death. On the contrary, he was filled with anticipation. He knew he would be with his Lord and that he would receive his reward—a crown of righteousness. He declared his fight of faith was over, and he had overcome.

Promise of reward for overcomers

Jesus told the apostle John that he who overcomes will receive a white stone with a name written on it, which no one knows except the one who receives it (Rev. 2:17). Jesus was talking to the church in the city of Pergamos, which had honored His name even in the place where Satan's throne was (v. 13). Yet some of them had compromised with the evil in that place, and He commanded them to repent. Then He promised that those who overcame would be rewarded—with a white stone.

Why a white stone? What kind of reward would that be? The people in Pergamos would have been very familiar with that term. There were several uses of the white stone that made it very significant to their lives.

Justification

The judicial system in that city had a special use for a white stone. When someone was accused of a crime, the defendant had to appear before a judge. The accuser would come and plead the case to the judge against him. After listening to both sides of the case, the judge would leave the courtyard for a time of deliberation. During that time the defendant was left standing in front of a pile of white stones with the people of the city standing around waiting for the judge's return.

When the judge walked back into the courtyard, every mouth was silenced and every eye was turned toward him. In his hand, the judge would either have a black stone, called the stone of condemnation, or a white stone, called the stone of justification.

If he handed the black stone to the defendant, the people of the city would pick up stones out of the pile and begin to stone him to death in the courtyard. But if he handed the accused one a white stone, it meant that all charges were dropped against him. The defendant was justified, found guiltless, and was to be released. They took off his chains and let him go free. He had been given the white stone of justification.[3]

Jesus promised a white stone to everyone who overcame the evil of their culture. Those who honored Christ and refused to compromise would be justified. And He personalized it. That white stone would have a name written on it that only the one who received it would know.

Someone has said that to be *justified* means to live in total freedom, "*just as if I'd* never sinned." What a heavenly reward Jesus promises to every believer! When your sins are covered by the blood of Jesus, you are justified, free from all guilt, as if you had never sinned! No more guilt! No more condemnation!

Victory

The white stone was also used in that culture to reward victory. When their armies came back from battle with another nation, the citizens of the city would line the streets to welcome home their war heroes. The king of the city would hand out white stones to the leaders in battle, which were equivalent to our medals of war.

Not everyone merits receiving a "white stone" medal, only those who fought the battle. That is a significant fact for every Christian seeking to live the fearless life. If you win the battle today, you will be promoted tomorrow. There is coming a day when every believer will stand before God to have his work judged. It will not determine whether or not you go to heaven. That is determined by your decision to be justified by the blood of Christ. But the judgment for your work will determine your reward.

God has an audit system. He will judge what you have built on the foundation of Jesus Christ. "Now if anyone builds on this foundation with gold, silver, precious stones, wood, hay, straw, each one's work will become clear; for the Day will declare it, because it will be revealed by fire; and the fire will test each one's work, of what sort it is" (1 Cor. 3:12–13).

When the fire burns up the wood, hay, and stubble, whatever remains will be rewarded. Some will be saved but have no reward for their works. It is important what you do in life to build the kingdom of God. Those who live quality lives in submission to the lordship of Christ will receive their reward. Compromise with the world will place your eternal reward in jeopardy.

Do you spend more time reading the Word of God or the TV guide? Are you fighting *for* your family or fighting *with* them? Do you invest your resources generously in the kingdom or lay up treasure for yourself? To receive a white stone of victory, you have to live a life surrendered to doing the will of God.

Citizenship

The white stone had another significant meaning besides justification and victory. For foreigners who were not born in Pergamos, there was the possibility of achieving citizenship through their noble actions. If a person showed loyalty to the king, he could be given the most highly prized gift the city could bestow on a person: the white stone of citizenship.

With that coveted reward, a person was immediately adopted as a citizen with all the rights of those who were born in that city. As a believer in Jesus Christ, we have received the white stone of citizenship as our reward. Our names are written in the Book of Life, and we have all the privileges of a citizen of heaven.

Do you want to spend eternity with the Lord in heaven? Do you want to live forever in a place where the streets are paved with gold, mansions are the dwelling places of the redeemed, God is the light, and where love and peace rule? Can you imagine a place where there are no tears, no pain or sorrow or death (Rev. 21:4)? Are you making yourself eligible for such eternal rewards?

A WHITE STONE OR A WHITE THRONE?

Heaven is a real place. Hell is a real place. You have two options for living forever in your life after death. You have the option of receiving the white stone of reward in heaven when you overcome. And you have the option of receiving damnation before the white throne of judgment. What will your choice be—the white stone or the white throne?

The apostle John saw a great white throne that was the throne of God. And he saw all the dead standing before it. Then he saw books, including the Book of Life, opened before them. The dead were judged according to what they had done in life, which was written in the books. Anyone whose name was not recorded in the Book of Life was thrown into the lake of fire (Rev. 20:11–15).

You do not have to fear death or eternity when you have believed in Jesus to cleanse you of your sins. Your name is written in the Book of Life. You have only to live in anticipation of the day you will receive your reward. The apostle Paul said that to be absent from the body is to be present with the Lord (2 Cor. 5:8). When you die, you will live in eternal bliss in the very presence of God.

But Jesus Himself said to fear the one who had the power to cast you into hell. When you stand before the white throne judgment, you won't be able to plead your case. The guilty verdict is already in place if your name is not found in the Book of Life. That is based on your choice in life to reject Christ. Your eternal fate will be to be cast into the lake of fire with the devil and his angels.

You don't have to face that awful fate. I remember

when I accepted Christ as my Savior. I walked into church knowing that I was a lost soul. I felt such guilt and condemnation when I heard the preached Word. Something inside of me said, "I can't take this anymore. I'm coming home to Jesus."

In that instant Jesus came to me like the good Samaritan. He knelt over my wounded soul and poured in His healing oil. He picked me up and led me to safety and paid my debt. He took care of me until I was made whole. And He is still taking care of me. He said to the Father, "Just put everything that he needs on My account. I have paid the price for all his sin."

That is the good news of the gospel. Jesus has paid the penalty for your sin, your failure, your addiction. He wants you to call on His name so that He can heal your wounds and set you totally free. Jesus will justify you, make you victorious, and offer you citizenship in heaven as your eternal home. When you make Him Lord of your life, He releases you from all fear of eternity and replaces it with anticipation of your reward.

MAKING THE MOST OF THE "DASH"

Jesus affirmed the existence of heaven and hell in His teachings. And He showed us how to escape from eternal damnation by accepting His sacrifice for our sins. If you have done that, you will have no fear of eternity. When you have settled your eternal destiny, what matters most is what you do with the dash.

Carved into a tombstone, there is usually a name and then dates—a beginning date and an ending date. Between those dates there is a little dash. Have you ever thought about the significance of that little dash?

It is a fact that you have no control over that beginning date. You did not choose when to be born. And you do not control the ending date either. No one chooses when to die. But you do have control over the dash between those dates. The years between the beginning and ending dates—the dash—represent your life. You are living the dash. How are you doing with your dash?

The Word of God teaches you how to make your

> When you make Jesus Lord of your life, He releases you from all fear of eternity and replaces it with anticipation of your reward.

life on earth most effective. After you accept Jesus as your Savior, God will reveal your personal destiny to you as you seek Him in prayer and in His Word. There is no greater joy, no greater liberty from the torment of fear, than when you learn to walk in the purpose of God for your life. That is when the dash becomes most effective and fulfilling. As a good steward of the gift of life God has given you, you will learn to build well on the foundation of Christ. And you will become eligible for the rewards of heaven He promises to those who overcome.

When your life is in the hands of Jesus Christ, death is not to be feared. He has the keys of death in His hands. For the one who is living the fearless life, death becomes simply a doorway to entering His presence, receiving your eternal reward, and living with Him forever and ever. You can overcome every fear that has tormented you when you surrender to His lordship.

If you want to experience glorious freedom from the fear of eternity, I encourage you to pray this prayer. As you do, you can expect to live a life totally free from fear:

Dear Lord Jesus, I accept forgiveness for my sins through the blood of Christ. And I give my life to You for Your purposes. I am determined to live a fearless life and to establish the kingdom of God in my life, in my family, in the church, and in the world. Thank You for giving me the promise of my eternal reward and for delivering me from the fear of eternity. Through Your grace, I know that my name is written in the Book of Life, and I will receive the white stone of the overcomer. Let me live in anticipation of my eternal home in heaven with You. Amen.

8

YOUR REFUGE FROM FEAR

WHERE DO YOU go when you need to feel safe? What do you do to get relief when you are facing threatening situations? Do you turn to food for comfort? Or alcohol? Or pills? Do you visit a psychiatrist? Or go to the mall or turn on the shopping channel for a spending spree?

Many people suffer from terrible addictions they have developed to try to cope with their fears. Some become workaholics. Others are addicted to media of various kinds. Some escape into TV, becoming couch potatoes. Many spend hours every day on the Internet, Facebook, Twitter, and Instagram. How do you escape the pressure and anxiety of your life?

I have good news for you. God has a safe place where you can live so that you don't have to be afraid. You don't have to escape into a dangerous addiction to get relief from your worry and fear. He wants to rescue you from every fear that torments your mind and emotions.

God wants to be your loving heavenly Father. He loves for His children to come running into His arms for comfort and protection. The Bible gives us beautiful pictures of this safe place. David wrote many of the psalms, but one of the most beautiful psalms about our refuge from fear was written by Moses.

In Psalm 91, which I've included in its entirety in the appendix of this book, Moses describes your safe place of freedom from fear and all the attacks of the enemy against your life. He calls it the "shadow of the Almighty." In modern language you could call it your very own home in God's presence. The good news is that when you run into God's shadow, He protects you from all harm with His great power. He wants you to know that you never have to live in fear again. That's the fearless life.

THE SHADOW OF THE ALMIGHTY

But what exactly is the shadow of the Almighty? The wilderness where Israel wandered for forty years was really an extremely hot desert. There was no shade there except what was provided by the tents in which the people lived. As a nomadic people, their only refuge from the burning sun was in the shadow of their tents. So they understood this powerful metaphor Moses used to describe their safe place in God—in the shadow of the Almighty.

To really appreciate what Moses was saying, you also need to understand the law of hospitality that God gave His people. It was a law that told them how to treat strangers who came into their camp.

If you were lost in the desert, were hungry, thirsty, or needed protection from an enemy, you could go into Israel's camp. The children of Israel were required to give you the help you needed because of the law of hospitality. The process was simple.

First, you had to find out the chief shepherd's name. Then you would go and grab the cord on his tent and begin to cry out for his help. When you did that, the law of hospitality required him to take you in and help you. You could find safety in the shadow of his tent.

All of Israel understood that when they took someone into their dwelling, they had to protect them with their life. Do you remember when angels went to rescue Lot from God's judgment on Sodom?

Lot invited the angels to come into his home. Then the wicked men of the city came to Lot's home. They threatened to destroy it if he did not let the angels come out so they could abuse them. Instead of giving in to these men, Lot offered them his virgin daughters. (See Genesis 19.)

As a father of four precious daughters, I could not fathom Lot's offer to trade his daughters for the well-being of the guests in his home. How could he allow his daughters to be violated by these wicked men? But the law of hospitality required Lot to protect those angels with his life. He had invited them into his home, and he was responsible for their safety. Lot had to do all in his power to rescue them from harm.

In Moses's song, he shows this same divine hospitality of God that will rescue you from fear. When you come into His presence and call on His name, He will go to all extremes to protect you from all evil.

God's name El Shaddai is translated into English as God Almighty. This describes His power to protect you—He has all power! He has the power of a lion to devour its prey and defend you against every enemy. El Shaddai is able to rescue you from all harm. All you have to do is call on His name and pull the cord of His tent.

CHRIST, OUR CHIEF SHEPHERD

Do you remember the woman with the issue of blood? She believed that if she could just touch the hem of Jesus's garment, she would be healed. What was that hem? It was the cord of the tent. She ran to Jesus to seek the healing she needed. When she touched His garment, Jesus knew someone had pulled on that cord. Immediately He turned to see who had touched Him.

The disciples were disgusted. They pointed out that with so many people in the crowd around Him, everyone was touching Him. But Jesus knew the difference between the jostling crowd and the touch of a woman who had run into His shadow. She had sought to touch Him with one purpose—the cry in her heart for His divine help. Jesus recognized her faith and pronounced her healed of her twelve-year sickness.

Do you need to be rescued from fear? From sickness? From financial problems? With tender love, Jesus will answer your cry for help. All of His power is at your disposal when you run to His shadow.

You can have all the promises Moses described in his song—in the name of Jesus. In Christ's shadow are healing and health, blessing and favor—and protection from all evil.

YOUR CITY OF REFUGE

God told Joshua to build six cities of refuge as safe places for the guilty to run into. According to the Law, it was legal for a family member to try to kill you to get justice for the person you killed. But when you killed someone accidentally, you could run to a city of refuge to hide. (See Joshua 20.)

When the leaders of the city were told what had happened, they were required to protect you from the vengeance of your enemy. The only stipulation was that you never leave that city of refuge until the high priest died. When that happened, you were free to go back to your family and take everything back you had lost because of your guilt.

Jesus Christ is called the High Priest of our confession (Heb. 3:1). When you run to Him to seek refuge, He asks you to confess what you have done. Then He offers you forgiveness and gives you His protection. He has paid for your pardon by taking all of your guilt to the cross of Calvary. He has set you free from everything your past says has a right to destroy you, judge you, and condemn you.

Christ will restore back to you everything you lost as a result of sin's power in your life. He is your High Priest. You can enter into a covenant of blessing on your life when you call on His name. As you learn to dwell in Christ, you can live the fearless life, free from the destructive power of sin.

Fearless in Spite of Attacks

Of course, God never promised you a life without problems. You cannot avoid the attacks of the enemy against your life. Before I bring this book to a close, I want to make sure you understand how to conquer his threats. There are three kinds of attacks the enemy uses to threaten you and your family.

The expected attack (the lion)

In Moses's song, he describes God's protection for you against the lion. I talked about the lion in an earlier chapter as a picture of an unequal fight, such as a life-threatening illness. But in Psalm 91 the lion also represents the threat of expected attacks against your life and family. When you are in the presence of a lion, you expect to be attacked. There are no surprises here. Life comes complete with built-in problems.

Are you facing relationship problems in your family, problems in your finances, your health, or your ministry? Then you need to receive God's divine protection from that expected attack of the lion.

The Bible refers to Satan as a roaring lion: "Be sober, be vigilant; because your adversary the devil walks about like a roaring lion, seeking whom he may devour" (1 Pet. 5:8). As a believer, you can expect that attacks of the enemy will come, no matter who you are. You should not be amazed— or afraid—when you are attacked because the Bible says it will happen.

Instead of giving in to fear, you have to stand up and call on the name of the Lord. He has promised to protect you when you do. Take a stand against the lion's plan for destruction. "Resist him, steadfast in the faith" (v. 9).

You don't have to fear the expected attack of the lion. God has promised you supernatural victory over every threat of the enemy. Run to His shadow, and use His wonderful name to overcome the enemy's expected attacks.

The unexpected attack (the snake)

Moses declared that God would protect you from snakes. An adder lies quietly under a rock or behind a bush and strikes when you least expect it. It represents the unexpected attack from the enemy. When you are attacked by an adder, you say things like, "Wow, I didn't see that coming!"—that accident, that job loss, that relational problem. "The adder was just lying there under that rock, and I did not see it coming to attack."

You know how frightening that unexpected attack can be. Somehow the element of surprise takes you off guard. You feel overwhelming fear in that moment. But you don't have to freak out when the adder attacks unexpectedly. Run to the shadow of El Shaddai. You need to know that miracles can strike as suddenly as tragedies! Just call on the name of the Lord!

Do what the apostle Paul did when the deadly snake grabbed his wrist, and shake it off into the fire. (See Acts 28.) When an adder attack of the enemy strikes you, don't just let it chew on you; shake it off!

If the adder tries to chew on your mind, filling it with fear, resentment, anger, or unforgiveness, shake it off. Don't allow him to gain advantage over you by listening to his sneaky accusations. The devil will try to steal your peace and joy, your relationships, and your faith in God. He will try to strike your children, your finances, and your future.

Run to the tent of El Shaddai, and allow Him to cleanse your heart from the chewing adder. He will destroy the traumatic effects of the unexpected attack on your life. God will restore to you all the enemy has tried to steal from you.

Satan is a joy robber. His unexpected attacks can chew away your joy. He wants you to get up every morning and hate your life. It can happen to any of us. Depression is always looming over us, but you don't have to take it. Just declare, "The Lord is my refuge. The Lord is my life. The Lord is my safe place." The Bible says that at His right hand there are pleasures forevermore (Ps. 16:11). God wants you to be a happy, carefree child living in His presence.

Satan wants to steal your peace. I prayed with a person who was being tormented by demon spirits. They kept him from sleeping at night, robbing him of his peace. I told him, "There is only one place where you can be safe. You can go to a psychiatrist, but they can't make you safe. You can try to get relief with medication or alcohol, but you will only find the true place of safety in the shadow of El Shaddai, God Almighty."

I know what it is to be attacked by devils. I have experienced this firsthand. But that is when I run to El Shaddai. I pull on His tent cord and call on His name. In that place of divine safety all the armies and angels of heaven step up and declare, "He's under the shadow of the Almighty! We have to rescue him!"

The unfounded attack (the dragon)

Moses also described God's protection for you from the fear of the dragon (Ps. 91:13, KJV). The dragon, in the original Hebrew language, referred to a marine or land monster, a whale, or a serpentine creature.

When I was a boy in school, I looked at maps of the early civilization that had pictures of dragons on them. The seamen who explored the world would not go to the places where the dragons were located. They were afraid to go beyond a certain point that had not been explored for fear of being devoured by a sea monster.

That is the way the devil tries to intimidate you. He keeps you from going beyond a certain point in your walk with God through fear of the unknown. Don't dream beyond this point. Don't reach for anything more, because the dragon will devour you. He hisses at you to keep you from pursuing your dream. But with God, there are no boundaries, just possibilities.

Because the children of Israel were in the middle of a desert, it seems highly improbable that they would have to face a dragon. Nevertheless, God wanted them to know they were protected from such a threatening beast.

This unlikely threat from the dragon represents your unfounded fears of attack. However remote the possibility of this attack, the enemy's threat can make you cower in your mind. You suffer the same pangs of worry and fear as though it will happen.

Unfounded attacks. Unfounded fears. You quiver inside and say, "I just know it's coming. I have been doing pretty good for a while, but I remember my daddy. He did OK for a while, and then he just kept messing up. I might be just like him."

Satan tries to plant all kinds of unfounded fear and worry in your mind over things that are highly improbable. He will tell you that you are going to lose it all, that your children are going to hell, or that you have cancer somewhere in your body. His goal is to make you cower before an unfounded fear. But God's power is greater than Satan's unfounded fears.

Only 8 percent of the things you worry about are even likely to happen. Most worry and fear are really much ado about nothing. Yet Satan is a master of painting pictures of impending disaster.

You see a plane crash on the evening television news, and you are scheduled to fly the next day. Your heart begins to pound, and you consider canceling your flight. Or a relative has a heart attack, and suddenly you feel like your heart is beating strangely. You need to change that devilish picture in your mind and run into the safety you have in Christ's shadow.

> Only 8 percent of the things you worry about are even likely to happen. Most worry and fear are really much ado about nothing.

Your unfounded fears may involve your personal relationships. You hear someone's conversation or think about the way they looked at you, and the devil will make you think everyone in the room is talking about you. Lighten up a little. You are not that important to everybody. (Speaking for myself, when I'm preaching, I don't meditate on any of my congregation's responses too long. If I did, I could have fifteen or twenty hits coming at me at the same time.) That is the dragon of fear painting unfounded pictures of disaster in your head.

You have to yell back at him with the truth of the Scriptures. Tell the devil you know that God loves you, no matter what people think of you. Declare to him that you are not going to fail. Use the Word of God and declare that you are being "transformed...from glory to glory" (2 Cor. 3:18). Tell the enemy that the Lord is the author and the finisher of your faith (Heb. 12:2). He is your El Shaddai, and that makes you fearless!

God did not promise you that you would never have any problems. But when problems come, He wants you to know that you never have to be afraid. You can be fearless in the midst of your problems. No fear can exist in His love when you dwell under His shadow.

God wants you to know that when you enter the protection of His shadow, He will go to all extremes to take care of you. It doesn't matter if you are dealing with the expected attack of the lion or the unexpected attack of the adder. It doesn't matter if you are facing fear of the unfounded attack of a dragon. Just call on the name of the Lord, and He will rescue you.

LIVING IN THE SHADOW OF SAFETY

We live in a world where there are threats of financial loss, random shootings, and child abduction. Divorce, drug addiction, cancer, atheistic New Age philosophies, nuclear destruction, and many other forms of evil taunt our lives.

It is not enough just to visit the shadow of God when you are in trouble. You have to make God's presence your very own home. The key to Moses's song is learning to dwell in the secret place, to abide under the shadow of the Almighty. To escape from the enemy's attacks, you need to follow biblical principles for living continually in the safety of God's shadow.

Confession

I tell my congregation often that "devil talk" will bring the devil on the scene, and "God talk" will bring God on the scene. There will always be things trying to attack you to pull you out of God's presence, out from under His shadow. But confessing the truth of the Word of God will keep you from giving in to the enemy's lies.

When you speak victory, you release the power of God for victory. When you speak defeat, that's what you will get. To live in the presence of God you have to confess the power of God to protect you and your family. You have to get some tent pegs from God's Word to drive into your mind and keep you speaking the truth. Declare the promises of God for your life.

Worship

The apostle Paul declared of Christ, "In Him we live and move and have our being" (Acts 17:28). God wants you to live in constant communion with Him. That is how you receive His constant provision and protection.

> Confessing the truth of the Word of God will keep you from giving in to the enemy's lies.

You cultivate communion by learning to worship God in spirit and in truth. Praising God and thanking Him for His love and provision keep you dependent on Him. You need to recognize that He is your source of life. That will keep you seeking Him and living under His shadow.

Moses did not have very peaceful circumstances

in his life. He led over two million people for forty years through the wilderness. The Bible says that the people complained and rebelled against him. At times they wanted to return to Egypt or get rid of Moses. Yet Moses is called the meekest man who ever lived.

How did he do it? He had learned to dwell in the presence of God. When he entered the tent to commune with God, all the people stood at their tent doors to see what God would do. They knew that he had learned to commune with God and to hear His voice.

The enemy knows whether you dwell in the shadow or just visit there when you are in trouble. He knows that his attacks are not successful when you are dwelling in the safety of God's presence. Your communion with God will keep you there.

Become a safe place

When God pours His life into you, refreshes and blesses you, He has a greater purpose than just your own welfare. He wants you to become a safe place, a "shadow on location" for someone else's desert experience. He will allow people to start pulling on the cord of your tent. Then He expects you to open your heart to them and pour into them the truth you have received.

God wants you to share with others the fearless life you have found in Christ. He will help you to lead them to Christ and to teach them how to dwell in His shadow. You will know the joy of seeing their lives set free from fear and the destructions of the enemy.

> You are delivered to bring deliverance to others! God wants to pour His life and power through you.

As Paul and Silas praised God at midnight in prison, God sent an earthquake that opened their prison doors. Yet they did not run away as free men. They stayed there and told the prisoners and the jailer about the wonderful freedom in Christ they had found. They led the jailer and his household to Christ.

You have to remember that you are delivered to bring deliverance to others! God wants to pour His life and power through you. He will use you to become a shadow on location to rescue your family, friends, and other precious lives from destruction.

I encourage you to learn to dwell under the shadow of the Almighty. Let your heart respond to the love of God, who wants to rescue you and keep you safe. Your responsibility is to call on His name and ask Him for His divine help.

> *Dear Lord Jesus, thank You for the safe place You have provided for me through Your death on Calvary and Your resurrection. Jesus, I call on Your name right now to help me. I surrender my life to Your care. Let me know You as my El Shaddai. Please become my shadow of the Almighty, my divine place of safety from evil. Teach me to live there in constant fellowship and communion with You. Then I ask You to make me a shadow on location to others who need to find a safe place in You. Thank You, Jesus. Amen.*

9

YOU HAVE FAITH for THIS!

WE HAVE ALL experienced fear that makes us want to draw back and play it safe. But people who overcome that fear are those who will make it in life. Now that you've read this book, my prayer is that you have decided to face life fearlessly. It doesn't mean you never feel afraid, but with God's help you won't let that feeling stop you from doing everything He has called you to do. When circumstances overwhelm you, when the fight seems unfair, you can stand with courage because God Almighty, El Shaddai, is on your side. He is for you, and He is your refuge from fear! When you are afraid, you can trust in Him. Whatever the challenge, nothing is impossible for those who are willing to live the fearless life of faith in God.

When God has asked me to do something that

seems impossible for me, do you know what I do? I preach to myself to defeat the fear and uncertainty that try to control me. When I am faced with an impossible task, when the job feels too big for me and I feel that I am out of my league, I preach three things to myself. They have helped me to redefine fearlessness and begin to live the fearless life. I encourage you to make these declarations over your situation.

JESUS IS WITH YOU

First, I preach this promise to myself: "Jesus is with me—and all power has been given to Him."

In one of the last conversations Jesus had with His disciples, He revealed to them that all power was given to Him in heaven and on earth. Then He gave them this promise: "Lo, I am with you always, even to the end of the age" (Matt. 28:18–20).

Jesus had just commanded these men to go to all the world to preach the gospel and make disciples. That must have seemed impossible to men who had never left their homeland. Jesus was telling them to do something that even He, the Christ, had never done.

Actually, the earthly ministry of Jesus never

covered much territory geographically. If you have ever visited Israel, you know that. You can travel from village to village easily in a few hours. His headquarters was in Capernaum, and He crossed the Sea of Galilee, but it is really just a lake. You can cross it in an hour.

Jesus never went to foreign soil. He never preached in a foreign nation. And yet He commanded His disciples to go into all the world. He left the whole job of winning the world to Christ to these few men.

Then He went up to heaven on a cloud-filled elevator—"See ya!"—and they were left standing there with a command to do what He never did. Their "impossible" job was to cover the whole earth with the good news of the gospel. But they also had this powerful promise from Jesus: "I am with you always, and I have all power. Wherever you go, I am there, even to the end of the world."

So, when you need to step out in faith for whatever challenge you face, preach to yourself, "Jesus is with me, and He has all power!" Jesus wants you to get that revelation. He is saying, "Hell couldn't keep Me, the grave couldn't hold Me, and demons couldn't trap Me. I am alive!" He looks at you and says, "Don't you back up. Don't you tremble. Don't be afraid! Fear not! I have all power!" All power belongs to God.

Your personal challenge is no greater than that of the disciples to go into all the world and make disciples. Whatever you have to face, that challenge is not in charge. It has no power over your life. If Jesus is in your life, He has all power over every challenge you face. You will never be immune to fear; you have to face it to become fearless.

When I get shaky and feel afraid and overwhelmed, I pull myself aside and start preaching to myself: "Jentezen, straighten up. Quit talking all that negative stuff. Jesus is with you, and all power is in His hands!"

> Whatever you have to face, that challenge is not in charge. It has no power over your life. If Jesus is in your life, He has all power.

Instead of talking fear, start declaring that the same Jesus who was with the three Hebrew boys in the fiery furnace is with you. When Nebuchadnezzar looked into the furnace and said, "Did we not cast three men bound into the midst of the fire?", those around him answered yes. He said, "I see four men...and the form of the fourth is like the Son of God" (Dan. 3:24–25).

I would like to correct him: "Mr. Nebuchadnezzar, He is not *like* the Son of God; He *is* the Son of God, and He is with me in my fiery furnace!" He has all power!

So, when you are afraid to take a risk, remember Jesus is with you! When your kids are in crisis, Jesus is with you! When you face overwhelming challenges in your finances, Jesus is with you! When you face challenges in the ministry, Jesus is with you! And He has all power in His hands!

GOD IS AT THE BOTTOM

You're probably thinking, "God is at the bottom. What does that mean?" Well, when I feel I have hit rock bottom and my challenges are too great for me to overcome, *God is there*. That's why the second thing I have learned to preach to myself is that no matter how low the trials of life take me, God is at the bottom.

Holocaust survivor Corrie ten Boom has been quoted as saying, "There is no pit so deep that God's love is not deeper still."[1] She was talking about the experience she and her sister, Betsie, faced in a Nazi concentration camp, which is about the deepest pit any human being has ever had to face. But what did she discover? God is there with you at your lowest point, and His love can save and keep you through the darkest, deepest times, no matter how desperate things become. God is at the bottom.

Moses talked to Israel at the close of his life about how great God is. In a kind of national address, he told them that there was no God like their God and that He rides the heavens to help them (Deut. 33:26). He described a God who is on top, above all, on high, a God who is great and mighty.

Do you remember the mighty miracles that God did on mountaintops? It was on Mount Moriah that God met with Abraham and Isaac and made His covenant of the blood of the lamb. On Mount Horeb Moses encountered the burning bush. It was on Mount Sinai that God gave the Ten Commandments. And on Mount Nebo Moses looked across and saw the Promised Land. It was on Mount Carmel that God sent fire down for Elijah.

God is a God of the high places; He is the God of mountaintop experiences. But Moses made a shift in focus right in the middle of telling about this great God of the high places. It is as though he was thinking, "I can't leave the people with the thought that God is only on top. He is not only with people when everything is victory, when everything is going right."

Then he said, "The eternal God is your refuge, and underneath are the everlasting arms" (Deut. 33:27). The Hebrew word for "underneath" means "bottom." So it could be translated, "God's arms are underneath you at the bottom." No matter how deep the valley you have to walk, God's presence is deeper. His arms are underneath you at the bottom.

We all know that God is at the top. But what you need to preach to yourself when you are facing fear and difficulty is that God is with you when you are at the bottom! You may look like you are down, but you cannot go so low in despair or depression, trouble or sorrow, that He is not there. When you feel that you can go no lower, underneath are His everlasting arms. God is not just the God of the top; He is also the God of the bottom!

I have learned that underneath everything I do in ministry are the everlasting arms of God. Underneath any crisis my family faces are the everlasting arms of God. Jesus is with me, and He has all power—not just when I am on top. God is underneath me, no matter how deep the challenge of trouble or pain. This comforting truth enables me to live fearlessly: God is at the bottom!

I encourage you to preach this to yourself as well. You may feel as though you are in a free fall sometimes. Financially you may be facing ruin. A doctor's report may have given you an "expiration date." Your family may be about to tear apart. You may have lost your best friend. Life may not seem worth living. When you feel as though you are at rock bottom, look for God in that place.

Let your faith declare that God is at the bottom. Underneath your lowest point, the arms of God are waiting to hold you up. When the dust settles, you will hear God say, "I am with you always!"

GOD HAS GIVEN EVERYONE A MEASURE OF FAITH

The third thing I preach to myself is the truth of God's Word that says, "God has dealt to each one a measure of faith" (Rom. 12:3). There is nothing that God will require of me for which I don't have the faith. He has given me the measure of faith I need to please Him. So whatever the challenge I am facing, I preach to myself, "I have faith for this."

Isaiah prophesied that God declares the beginning

from the end and from ancient times things that are not yet done (Isa. 46:10). God establishes your end and then goes back to you to say, "OK, let's begin. If you stay in faith, you will walk in My plan for your life because it is already established. I established your end from the beginning."

God has given you the faith you need to begin to walk in His will. Jesus is with you, and He has all power. So when fear threatens your victory, remember these simple truths about faith.

1. Faith is important.

First, faith is important. Jesus said to Simon Peter, "Simon, Simon! Indeed, Satan has asked for you, that he may sift you as wheat. But I have prayed for you, that your faith should not fail" (Luke 22:31–32). That was the most important prayer Jesus could pray for Simon.

It is the most important prayer for you also. Not a prayer that you would have the best financial year of your life. Not that you have a life without trouble or problems. But prayer that your faith does not fail.

Faith is more important than money. It is more important than a successful career. It is more important than happiness. Why? Because if you take everything I have but leave me with my faith,

I will be back! Faith will connect me to God's will. God is always with me, and He has all power. Failure will never be final if my faith does not fail.

Jesus was saying, in effect, "When Satan is attacking you, the most important prayer that I can pray for you is that your faith will stand through this process you are going through, that your faith will not fail!" Remember first of all that faith is important.

2. It doesn't take huge faith.

The second thing about faith is that you don't have to have a lot of it to live fearlessly. Jesus said that faith the size of a mustard seed was enough to move a mountain. Then He said that with that kind of faith, nothing would be impossible to you (Matt. 17:20).

Faith is more important than money. It is more important than a successful career. It is more important than happiness.

The "mustard seed" concept was a phrase used in Jesus's day to describe something insignificant and small. But Jesus elevated it to say that you need only that "insignificant" kind of faith to do the impossible. Don't despise the day of small beginnings. Let your faith work like that little mustard seed.

You see, the tiny mustard seed has an innate power to grow and overcome obstacles to become a mighty tree. It presses up through the dark earth, around rocks, braving storms and avoiding animals and other threats to its life. It is not so much the size of your faith but the quality of faith that you need to succeed.

It just takes "mustard seed" faith to move something from the impossibility column to the possibility column. The only thing standing between your impossibility and your possibility is a mustard seed kind of faith.

I need this little truth about faith. You see, I don't have great faith. Every time we need to expand the ministry, purchase another TV station, or do whatever God says to do, I just take my little grain of mustard seed faith out there. It has to press through the obstacles.

I make the decisions that are needed and feel as though I am obeying God. Then when the bills start coming in, I feel fear rising, and I start praying, "O God, what are we going to have to cut to make this happen?" But instead of giving in to that fear,

I begin to preach to myself that Jesus is with me, that He has all power, and that He has given me a measure of faith to do all His will. My mustard seed faith grows a little more and overcomes the fear.

You need to let your mustard seed faith grow and increase to become a large tree that flourishes and conquers every fear. It is a faith that doesn't give up. Mustard seed faith is unconquerable faith; it is faith that won't quit. Don't quit in the face of adversity. Call on your faith, and watch it overcome every obstacle.

"I HAVE FAITH FOR THIS!"

So when I'm preaching to myself and I get to the third point about faith, "God has given me a measure of faith," I often say it this way: "I have faith for this!" This statement is powerful for the person living the fearless life.

Because He has given me a measure of faith and He is asking me to do a certain thing, even if all I have is a mustard seed kind of faith, nevertheless, "I have faith for this!" That is what I preach to myself when something impossible threatens to defeat my family or an area of ministry: *I have faith for this.*

When you are facing a bad report from a doctor

or your money is acting funny, just say, "I have faith for this." When the devil is showing you a big zero for your future, just laugh at him and say, "Jesus is with me, and He has all power. God is at the bottom, and underneath are His everlasting arms—and I have faith for this."

I pray that you can preach these things to yourself as I do to help you to fight fear effectively. Declare right now:

1. Jesus is with me, and He has all power!

2. God is at the bottom!

3. I have faith for this!

It is not God's will for your life to be ruled by fear of any kind. Yet fear is one of the greatest evils you must face and defeat! To live a fearless life in a world driven by fear, you must submit your life to the lordship of Christ. As you seek first the kingdom of God and His righteousness (Matt. 6:33), you will be restored to intimate relationship with God. Then you can learn to fight fear with the promises of God's Word.

To live a fearless life, you will need God's arsenal of divine weapons. Without these divine weapons you cannot defeat fear. It is impossible to discuss every divine weapon in God's arsenal in this book. You can trust the Holy Spirit to teach you to become effective in facing your fears. As you progress, you will discover more and more divine weapons in the Word of God to use against the power of fear in your life.

You may be at a point in your life right now where God has told you to do a hard thing. You know you have heard from God, and you are moving in faith. But you have started to feel the cold feet syndrome. Let me encourage you: be of good courage; the Lord is with you! Begin to declare, "Jesus is with me, and He has all power. I have faith for this!"

As you take these steps to living the fearless life, you will discover that many of your worst fears have actually been "much ado about nothing." You will learn to live in the wonderful shelter of safety that God provides for you. If you have decided to live the fearless life, please pray this prayer with me:

> *Dear heavenly Father,*
> *I come to You to declare the truth that Jesus is with me, and He has all power. I declare that You are the God at*

the bottom when I feel like life is over and I cannot go on. I choose to believe that I have faith for this, that You have given me a measure of faith to live the fearless life—and win! I submit my life completely to Your lordship, Jesus. I choose to face my fears and learn to live a life of victory over all fear. Thank You, Lord. Amen.

Appendix

MOSES'S SONG of DIVINE SAFETY

You who sit down in the High God's
   presence,
   spend the night in Shaddai's shadow,
Say this: "GOD, you're my refuge.
   I trust in you and I'm safe!"
That's right—he rescues you from hidden
   traps,
   shields you from deadly hazards.
His huge outstretched arms protect you—
   under them you're perfectly safe;
   his arms fend off all harm.
Fear nothing—not wild wolves in the
   night,
   not flying arrows in the day,
Not disease that prowls through the
   darkness,
   not disaster that erupts at high noon.
Even though others succumb all around,
   drop like flies right and left,
   no harm will even graze you.

You'll stand untouched, watch it all from
a distance,
watch the wicked turn into corpses.
Yes, because GOD's your refuge,
the High God your very own home,
Evil can't get close to you,
harm can't get through the door.
He ordered his angels
to guard you wherever you go.
If you stumble, they'll catch you;
their job is to keep you from falling.
You'll walk unharmed among lions and
snakes,
and kick young lions and serpents
from the path.
"If you'll hold on to me for dear life," says
GOD,
"I'll get you out of any trouble.
I'll give you the best of care
if you'll only get to know and trust me.
Call me and I'll answer, be at your side in
bad times;
I'll rescue you, then throw you a party.
I'll give you a long life,
give you a long drink of salvation!"
—PSALM 91, THE MESSAGE

NOTES

INTRODUCTION

1. Harvey Mackay, "Worrying Makes You Cross the Bridge Before You Come to It," HarveyMackay .com, June 11, 2012, http://tinyurl.com/l3v9kjy (accessed August 5, 2013).
2. Author unknown, "Risk," SermonIllustrations .com, http://www.sermonillustrations.com/a-z/r/ risk.htm (accessed August 5, 2013).

CHAPTER 2
FEARLESS ABOUT FAILURE

1. Child Development Institute, "Helping Your Child Deal With Fears and Phobias," http://childdevelop mentinfo.com/child-psychology/anxiety_disor ders_in_children/fears/ (accessed August 5, 2013).
2. Ronald Rood, as quoted in John Cook, Steve Deger, and Leslie Ann Gibson, *The Book of Positive Quotations* (Minneapolis, MN: Fairview Press, 2007), 482.
3. BrainyQuote.com, "Thomas Edison Quotes," http://www.brainyquote.com/quotes/quotes/t/ thomased132683.html (accessed August 5, 2013).
4. Jacques Pepin, "Burger Meister RAY KROC," *TIME*, December 7, 1998, http://www.time.com/ time/magazine/article/0,9171,989785,00.html (accessed August 5, 2013).

5. Ron Kurtus, "Failures of Abraham Lincoln (1800s)," School for Champions, October 11, 2011, http://www.school-for-champions.com/history/lincoln_failures.htm (accessed August 5, 2013).

6. "'Professor' Albert Einstein Unmasked at Last!," http://www.reformation.org/einstein-unmasked.html (accessed August 5, 2013).

7. "Sir Roger Bannister," Answers.com, http://www.answers.com/topic/roger-bannister (accessed August 5, 2013).

8. QuoteWorld.com, http://www.quoteworld.org/quotes/10767 (accessed August 5, 2013).

9. "Biography of Nathaniel Hawthorne," GradeSaver.com, http://www.gradesaver.com/author/hawthorne (accessed August 5, 2013).

10. BBC.com, "Lions," http://www.bbc.co.uk/dna/ptop/alabaster/A12921428 (accessed August 5, 2013).

Chapter 3
Fearless About People

1. Adapted from "The Ben Hooper Story: Who's Your Daddy?," which can be found on various sites on the Internet.

Chapter 4
Fearless About Having Enough

1. Amarnath Tewary, "India's Poor Urged to 'Eat Rats,'" BBCNews.com, August 13, 2008, http://news.bbc.co.uk/2/hi/south_asia/7557107.stm (accessed August 6, 2013).

CHAPTER 6
FEARLESS ABOUT YOUR HEALTH

1. Bob Glassner, *The Culture of Fear* (Philadelphia: Basic Books, 1999), xx.
2. Ibid.
3. Ibid.
4. QuotationsPage.com, "Dorothy Bernard Quotes," http://www.quotationspage.com/quote/29699.html (accessed August 6, 2013).
5. GoodReads.com, "Mark Twain > Quotes > Quotable Quote," http://tinyurl.com/a7rw87z (accessed August 6, 2013).

CHAPTER 7
FEARLESS ABOUT DEATH AND ETERNITY

1. "Anxiety and Fear," Encyclopedia of Death and Dying, http://www.deathreference.com/A-Bi/Anxiety-and-Fear.html (accessed August 6, 2013).
2. Deepak Chopra, "The Six Most Feared but Least Likely Causes of Death," SixWise.com, http://www.sixwise.com/newsletters/05/07/13/the_six_most_feared_but_least_likely_causes_of_death.htm (accessed August 6, 2013).
3. Sam Storms, "The Letter to the Church at Pergamum," Enjoying God Ministries, November 5, 2006, http://tinyurl.com/ktr276d (accessed August 6, 2013).

CHAPTER 9
YOU HAVE FAITH FOR THIS!

1. CorrietenBoom.com, "History," http://www
.corrietenboom.com/history.htm (accessed August
6, 2013). This is something her sister, Betsie, told
her while they were in Ravensbruck: "We must
tell them that there is no pit so deep that He is
not deeper still." [Corrie ten Boom, *The Hiding
Place* (Grand Rapids, MI: Chosen Books, 1974,
1984), 227.]

Enjoy these additional messages
from *New York Times* best-selling author

Jentezen Franklin